Effective Mentoring in Initial Teacher Education

DEDICATION

We are grateful to the ITE providers with whom we have been employed, and their partnerships, which have informed these approaches to mentoring.

ACKNOWLEDGEMENTS

We wish to acknowledge specifically the School of Education at the University of Hull. The university's approach to mentoring and ITE curriculum development has underpinned some of the ideas in this book.

To order our books please go to our website www.criticalpublishing.com or contact our distributor Ingram Publisher Services, telephone 01752 202301 or email IPSUK.orders@ingramcontent.com. Details of bulk order discounts can be found at www.criticalpublishing.com/delivery-information.

Our titles are also available in electronic format: for individual use via our website and for libraries and other institutions from all the major ebook platforms.

Effective Mentoring in Initial Teacher Education

Jonathan Glazzard and Michael Green

First published in 2024 by Critical Publishing Ltd

All rights reserved. No part of this publication may be reproduced, stored in a retrieval system, or transmitted in any form or by any means, electronic, mechanical, photocopying, recording or otherwise, without prior permission in writing from the publisher.

The authors have made every effort to ensure the accuracy of information contained in this publication, but assume no responsibility for any errors, inaccuracies, inconsistencies and omissions. Likewise, every effort has been made to contact copyright holders. If any copyright material has been reproduced unwittingly and without permission the Publisher will gladly receive information enabling them to rectify any error or omission in subsequent editions.

Copyright © 2024 Jonathan Glazzard and Michael Green

British Library Cataloguing in Publication Data
A CIP record for this book is available from the British Library

ISBN: 978-1-915713-87-2

This book is also available in the following e-book formats:

EPUB ISBN: 978-1-915713-88-9
Adobe e-book ISBN: 978-1-915713-89-6

The right of Jonathan Glazzard and Michael Green to be identified as the Authors of this work has been asserted by them in accordance with the Copyright, Design and Patents Act 1988.

Text and cover design by Out of House Limited
Project Management by Newgen Publishing UK

Critical Publishing
3 Connaught Road
St Albans
AL3 5RX

www.criticalpublishing.com

CONTENTS

MEET THE AUTHORS PAGE VII

INTRODUCTION PAGE 1

01
PAGE 4

The ITE policy context

02
PAGE 17

Principles, models and approaches to generic mentoring

03
PAGE 31

The ITE curriculum and implications for mentors

04
PAGE 48

Inclusive mentoring

05
PAGE 64

Subject- and phase-specific mentoring

06
PAGE 78

Subject-specific feedback: a toolkit for mentors

07
PAGE 99

Assessing trainee progress and target setting

08
PAGE 110

Educational research for mentors

09
PAGE 124

Supporting trainees' workload and mental health

10
PAGE 141

Mentoring early career teachers

CONCLUSION PAGE 156

REFERENCES PAGE 158

INDEX PAGE 171

MEET THE AUTHORS

JONATHAN GLAZZARD

Jonathan Glazzard's research focuses on mental health, wellbeing and inclusion in education. He holds the Rosalind Hollis Chair in Education for Social Justice at the University of Hull. Jonathan is a co-convenor of the British Educational Research Association (BERA) Special Interest Group: Mental Health and Wellbeing in Education. He has published widely on aspects of inclusion and social justice for marginalised groups and individuals, and he is deeply committed to research-informed teaching and to research that improves the lives of individuals.

MICHAEL GREEN

Michael Green has over 22 years' experience in education, holding a number of senior positions in a range of settings. These include executive leadership within a large multi-academy trust as Director of Strategy and Projects, working for Ofsted as one of His Majesty's Inspectors of Education, leading initial teacher education and partnership development in higher education, working as a government adviser in the Department for Education, undertaking international advisory work on curriculum and teacher development, and senior leadership positions within primary schools.

INTRODUCTION

School-based mentoring has long played an important role in Initial Teacher Training (ITT) and Initial Teacher Education (ITE) in England for several decades. During the 1980s, mentoring became an important feature of early university–school partnerships in England (McIntyre, 1990). In the early 1990s, new government policies in England (DfE, 1992, 1993) increased the amount of time that trainee teachers were required to spend in schools, and it was stipulated that, during this time, they should be supported by a mentor. Mentoring subsequently became a feature of the induction year for teachers during their first year of teaching. Recent policy changes since 2020, including the initial teacher education inspection framework (Ofsted, 2020), and other policy frameworks which we outline in Chapter 1, have led to an even greater emphasis on mentoring during both ITT and the early career phase.

The role of the school-based mentor is a dual role. Mentors *develop* trainee teachers through a range of mentoring approaches but, at the same time, they also *assess* the trainee's progress towards professional competencies. Hobson and Malderez (2013) coined the term *judgementoring* to capture this dualistic nature of mentoring. However, when mentors too readily make negative judgements on trainees the roles of mentor and assessor can be conflicting.

From September 2024, ITT providers in England are required by law to implement new regulations which will have a significant impact on mentoring within the ITT/ITE context. Mentors will be required to complete significantly more training, which reflects the increasing significance of the mentor role within ITT/ITE. In addition, ITE partnerships must recruit and develop *lead mentors* and ITE providers must develop Intensive Training and Practice opportunities which have a tightly defined focus. Chapter 1 outlines these key developments.

The remaining chapters of this book focus on approaches to mentoring, assessment, feedback and target setting. We also address mentoring within the context of the early career phase. The book also provides practical guidance to support mentors in providing trainees with subject-specific feedback.

Perhaps one of the most significant developments within the ITE/ITT context in England is the disruption of the theory–practice divide. The misconceived view that trainees learned the theory of teaching through centre-based training, often in a university, and then applied this in schools during periods of teaching practice is not the model that ITE/ITT partnerships are following. Trainees develop their knowledge of educational policy, theory and pedagogy through an ITE curriculum which is implemented in centre-based provision *and* in schools through training by expert mentors. Trainees can also learn the practical skills of teaching in both contexts. The new policy climate requires partnerships to develop greater synergy between what trainees learn in the centre and what they learn in schools (and vice versa). School-based training and centre-based training should build on the knowledge that has been gained in the other context so that trainees know more, remember more and can do more as they move from one context to the other. Teachers and leaders from partnership schools must take an active role in designing the curriculum in the centre and in schools, and expert mentors should regularly contribute to the implementation of training in the centre. The relationships between ITE providers and their schools must be symbiotic so that trainees experience a well-sequenced and coherent curriculum.

TERMINOLOGY

This book uses a range of terminology. These are outlined below.

Early career teacher (ECT): Currently, the ECT is a two-year phase post qualification in England. ECTs follow a two-year programme of professional learning and development, delivered by an accredited provider.

Initial Teacher Education (ITE): This is the phase which leads to qualification as a teacher. Typically, trainees study a one-year postgraduate qualification or three-year undergraduate degree programme which leads to qualification as a teacher. Training may take place in universities, but also in SCITTs (School-Centred Initial Teacher Training providers).

Initial Teacher Training and Early Career Framework (ITTECF): This is the regulatory framework which sets out the minimum content for ITT courses and early career framework providers which provide professional development for early career teachers (ECTs).

ITAP: Intensive Training and Practice opportunities.

INTRODUCTION

ITE partnerships: A partnership is an arrangement between an ITE provider and its schools.

Initial Teacher Training (ITT): This is an alternative to ITE.

Lead mentor: Lead mentors are mentors who adopt an enhanced role in curriculum design, curriculum implementation and quality assurance.

Mentor: Mentors are usually (but not exclusively) experienced teachers who support, develop and assess trainee teachers in schools during periods of teaching practice.

Ofsted: This is the Office for Standards in Education, Children's Services and Skills. It is an independent regulatory body which inspects schools and ITE partnerships.

Trainee teacher/trainees: These are pre-service teachers who are following a programme of professional training and education to qualify as a teacher.

CHAPTER 1
THE ITE POLICY CONTEXT

CHAPTER OBJECTIVES

By the end of this chapter you will understand:

+ the ITE policy context in England;
+ the implications of this policy context for mentors.

INTRODUCTION

This chapter provides an overview of the Initial Teacher Training and Education policy context in England. ITT/ITE is a heavily regulated sector in England. Various regulatory frameworks exist which regulate accreditation, recruitment and selection of trainees, curriculum design, assessment, partnerships and mentoring. However, despite centralised regulation of what trainees should learn and how ITT partnerships should operate, ITE providers in England still have a degree of autonomy in determining, to some extent, the content of their ITT curriculums, the content of mentor training and the structure and content of placements, providing that the minimum regulatory requirements have been met. This chapter covers some of the key changes which must be in place by September 2024 for ITE providers in England.

THE INITIAL TEACHER TRAINING AND EARLY CAREER FRAMEWORK

The Initial Teacher Training and Early Career Framework (DfE, 2024a) was developed by combining two separate frameworks: the ITT Core

CHAPTER 1: THE ITE POLICY CONTEXT

Content Framework (DfE, 2019a) and the Early Career Framework (DfE, 2019b). The Framework states:

The ITTECF sets out the entitlement of every trainee and early career teacher (ECT) to the core body of knowledge, skills and behaviours that define great teaching, and to the mentoring and support from expert colleagues they should receive throughout the three or more years at the start of their career.

(DfE, 2024a, p 4)

The Framework boldly claims that it is '*informed by the best available educational research*' (p 5) and emphasises that it is a *minimum* entitlement to training and not a full curriculum. The '*Learn that*' and '*Learn how to*' statements which form the basis of the Framework are intended to be revisited during the ITT phase and ECT phase to deepen understanding. ITT providers and their partnerships are required to develop a well-sequenced, coherent curriculum which specifies the content that will be delivered by the training provider and the content that will be delivered by mentors and other expert teachers in schools. ITT providers and mentors should be clear about the content that is being delivered by the provider and in schools to reduce unnecessary repetition.

The following case study provides an example to illustrate how content may be delivered in different settings.

CASE STUDY

MEMORY

The **ITE provider** is responsible for addressing the following statements from Standard 2 'How Pupils Learn' in the Framework.

LEARN THAT …

- An important factor in learning is memory, which can be thought of as comprising two elements: working memory and long-term memory. (Standard 2)

→

- Working memory is where information that is being actively processed is held, but its capacity is limited and can be overloaded. (Standard 2)
- Long-term memory can be considered as a store of knowledge that changes as pupils learn by integrating new ideas with existing knowledge. (Standard 2)

These aspects are delivered through centre-based training. Trainees are introduced to a model of memory. They learn that working memory is made up of several components, which process different types of information. Trainees learn that working memory is limited in capacity and that individuals experience cognitive load when working memory reaches its capacity. Trainees learn about different types of cognitive load, including intrinsic load, extraneous load and germane load. They learn that working memory processes new information, and that information then transfers to long-term memory for storage.

Through the ITE curriculum in school, trainees learn the following content from the Framework.

LEARN HOW TO ...

- Taking into account pupils' prior knowledge when planning how much new information to introduce. (Standard 2)
- Breaking complex material into smaller steps (eg using partially completed examples to focus pupils on the specific steps). (Standard 2)
- Identifying pupils who need new content further broken down. (Standard 5)

The mentor shows the trainee an example of a lesson plan which introduces pupils to knowledge about electricity in science. The mentor explains what the pupils learned before this lesson and explains how this lesson connects to, and builds on, prior learning. The mentor then guides the trainee to plan the next science lesson. They explain the importance of limiting the amount of new knowledge that is being introduced and support the trainee to break the content down into smaller steps. The trainee then teaches the lesson, and the mentor observes this. Following the lesson, the mentor returns to the statements in the Framework and asks the trainee to reflect on which pupils need the content to be broken down further.

CRITICAL QUESTIONS

+ How does the ITE curriculum in school support the curriculum in the centre?
+ What alternative mentoring approaches might the mentor use to implement the school-based components of the ITE curriculum in this example?

THE ITT MARKET REVIEW

The UK government controversially implemented a Market Review in 2021 (DfE, 2021). The review was implemented due to concerns about quality in the sector, which are summarised below:

+ *Too few partnerships had a sufficiently ambitious curriculum.*
+ *ITE curricula were underpinned by outdated or discredited theories of education and not well enough informed by the most pertinent research.*
+ *Alignment between centre-based and school-based training was not always well-considered.*

(DfE, 2021, p 8)

Many recommendations from the Market Review became statutory requirements in the 2024 ITT criteria (DfE, 2024b). These requirements are outlined throughout this chapter.

THE ACCREDITATION PROCESS

The ITT Market Review resulted in the introduction of a controversial accreditation process. ITE providers in England that wished to continue training teachers, or new providers that wished to offer training post 2024, were required to pass an accreditation process. A significant number of providers did not meet the required standards on their first submission and were allowed to re-apply for accreditation. Some providers were not granted accreditation on the second submission and were either forced to partner with a successful provider or exit the market. Some providers chose to exit the market, resulting in concerns being raised about teacher supply.

CRITICAL QUESTIONS

+ What are the advantages of the accreditation process?
+ What are the disadvantages of the process?

2024 ITT REQUIREMENTS

The outcomes of the Market Review informed the development of the statutory ITT criteria (DfE, 2024b). Providers must ensure compliance with the criteria. Within the criteria there is an emphasis on mentor training, the role of mentors and Intensive Training and Practice opportunities. These are outlined below.

THE EMPHASIS ON MENTORING

According to the Market Review:

+ *There is strong evidence that effective mentoring is critical to high-quality ITT.*
+ *Mentors require focused and evidence-informed training, as well as ongoing support and knowledge of the training curriculum.*
+ *Mentors require subject-specific and phase-specific professional development.*

(DfE, 2021)

The Ofsted inspection framework (Ofsted, 2020), the Initial Teacher Training and Early Career Framework (ITTECF) (DfE, 2024a) and the ITT regulations (DfE, 2024b) all emphasise the importance of mentoring. To be compliant with the ITT criteria, mentors should have a clear understanding of the mentor's role and skills, the ITT Core Content Framework, and the ITT curriculum and evidence that underpins it (DfE, 2024b). Mentors should use the techniques of observation, reflection and deconstruction to support the trainee's development and all mentors must ensure that in-school experiences are coherent with the ITT curriculum. Mentors should provide trainees with opportunities for purposeful practice and high-quality feedback. These approaches are outlined in Chapter 2.

CRITICAL QUESTIONS

+ What challenges do large ITE partnerships experience in relation to mentoring?
+ How might ITE partnerships address these challenges?

MENTOR TRAINING

According to the ITT criteria:

+ *Mentor training builds mentors' knowledge and understanding of the ITT curriculum, and the evidence that underpins it.*
+ *Training can be delivered face to face or virtually. Some use of asynchronous training may also be appropriate.*

(DfE, 2024b)

The ITT criteria stipulates the minimum time allocations for mentor training which providers must meet. ITT providers are required to design a mentoring curriculum which outlines the essential knowledge that mentors need to learn to carry out their roles. Providers generally offer different types of mentor training. These include:

+ training for all mentors on the generic principles of mentoring;
+ subject-specific mentor training to support the development of mentors' subject knowledge, including how to provide trainees with subject-specific feedback and targets;
+ training for lead mentors;
+ training for specific placements, eg Intensive Training and Practice opportunities.

It is important that ITT providers ensure that there are well-established, seamless systems which ensure that mentors can receive ongoing support. Mentor training will need to include content on the ITE curriculum and content that introduces mentors to the research evidence in the ITTECF (DfE, 2024a).

LEAD MENTORS

The 2024 criteria include a specific requirement for providers to develop the role of the lead mentor. The roles of lead mentors may include:

+ *oversight, supervision and quality assurance of other mentors;*
+ *design and delivery of training for other mentors;*
+ *close working with trainees during Intensive Training and Practice, and design of such elements;*
+ *oversight of trainee progress through the year and identification of interventions or modifications where required.*

(DfE, 2024b, p 32)

Providers are responsible for recruiting lead mentors and identifying the criteria for recruitment to the role. Lead mentors should have a deep knowledge of the ITE curriculum and its underpinning evidence base. They may take a lead role in designing Intensive Training and Practice opportunities, for training other mentors and for implementing quality assurance processes. Lead mentors may also contribute to delivery of centre-based training, and they may lead training for groups of trainees in schools.

INTENSIVE TRAINING AND PRACTICE OPPORTUNITIES

Intensive Training and Practice opportunities (ITAPs) must be embedded within all ITT programmes in England from September 2024. Providers can determine the curriculum content of an ITAP. This may relate to the ITTECF (DfE, 2024a), although this is not a strict requirement.

Minimum time requirements are stated in the 2024 criteria. Each ITAP provides trainees with an opportunity to learn about a very focused aspect of teaching. It is for providers to determine how to organise and structure the ITAPs, and training can take place within the centre and in schools. Focus areas of Intensive Training and Practice should:

+ be pivotal or foundational concepts of the planned ITT curriculum that trainees can put into practice immediately;
+ be granular in nature;

- have potential to impact on trainees' classroom practice irrespective of context;
- include three to five carefully selected pivotal or foundational aspects of the planned curriculum. These will be identified in the overall design of the ITT curriculum;
- provide opportunities for structured observation of selected teaching practice;
- provide opportunities for critical analysis of observed teaching and relevant teaching materials, guided by an expert;
- include preparation for, and implementation of, classroom teaching practice with deliberate attention to the aspects under focus, and with expert feedback;
- include expert theoretical and practical input by tutor(s) and/ or mentor(s) and other expert colleagues (in school or in an ITT institution);
- include focused observation, reflection upon and deconstruction of teaching;
- include expert modelling and deconstruction of individual components of teaching practice;
- include live classroom teaching practice (or practice in a rehearsal environment), with deliberate attention to the aspects under focus (in school);
- include focused feedback utilising appropriate questioning and opportunities to practise further and improve.

CRITICAL QUESTIONS

- What would make a good focus for an ITAP?
- What are the advantages of including ITAPs in an ITT programme?
- What challenges might ITT providers experience in implementing ITAPs?
- How might these challenges be overcome?

CASE STUDY

EXAMPLE OF AN ITAP: MANAGING TRANSITIONS

Table 1.1 shows how an ITAP might be structured. The ITT provider decided to focus on managing children's transitions to facilitate good behaviours.

Table 1.1 Structuring an ITAP

Phase of the ITAP	Implementation
1	**Day 1: Modelling and deconstruction** **Modelling:** In the centre-based training session observe using recorded lessons how teachers manage the following transitions: + children entering the class and sitting down; + children lining up to go to assembly; + moving children from one activity to another in the classroom, for example, from the carpet area to tables; + children getting changed for physical education. **Deconstruct:** Discuss with the trainees how the teachers minimise disruption. Unpack what the teacher is *doing* in each scenario to ensure that transitions are smooth. Consider how the teachers: + use rewards and sanctions; + provide manageable, specific and sequential instructions; + use consistent language and non-verbal signals;

CHAPTER 1: THE ITE POLICY CONTEXT

Table 1.1 (Continued)

Phase of the ITAP	Implementation
	+ set and reinforce expectations about key transition points; + provide repeated opportunities for children to practise. Trainees are introduced to Bruner's work on scaffolding, and this is applied to transitions.
2	**Day 2: Structured observation** Trainees in school observe a variety of transitions during the day. They record their observations in a notebook. These observations are guided by a mentor.
3	**Day 2: Guided reflection of observed teaching** The mentor meets with trainees to review their observations. The mentor uses the following questions to guide trainee reflections: + What different transitions did you observe? + How did the teachers prepare children for the transitions? + When transitions were smooth, what did the teachers do to ensure this? + What did the teachers do when transitions did not run smoothly? + What are the implications for your own teaching? For example: a) when moving the children from the carpet to tables; b) when children are entering the classroom; c) when children are leaving the classroom; d) when the children are getting changed for physical education.
4	**Day 3: Deliberate practice** Trainees plan for taking a class into assembly and returning them back to class. Trainees deliberately practise what they have learned about transitions so far. Expert mentors observe the trainees.

→

Table 1.1 (Continued)

Phase of the ITAP	Implementation
5	**Day 3: Observation and feedback** Mentors use guided reflection to support the trainees to reflect on their practice and link their learning in school back to the theory that was shared with trainees on Day 1.

CRITICAL QUESTIONS

+ What aspects of the ITTECF are covered through this ITAP?
+ What additional experiences might you provide to deepen trainees' knowledge of managing transitions?

LEAD PARTNERS

Lead partnerships replace School Direct partnerships from September 2024. Lead partners work in collaboration with accredited ITT providers to support the following aspects of ITT delivery:

+ trainee recruitment;
+ delivering ITT courses;
+ curriculum design;
+ designing and delivering of mentor curriculums;
+ supplying lead mentors;
+ running ITAP opportunities;
+ quality assurance of key aspects including mentoring.

RESEARCH

Rosenshine (2012) identified the following principles of effective instruction:

+ Begin a lesson with a short review of previous learning.
+ Present new material in small steps with student practice after each step.

- Ask many questions and check the responses of all students.
- Provide models.
- Guide student practice.
- Check for student understanding.
- Obtain a high success rate.
- Provide scaffolds for difficult tasks.
- Require and monitor independent practice.
- Engage students in weekly and monthly review.

CRITICAL QUESTIONS

Some of these principles may also support effective mentoring practice.

- How might mentors use modelling?
- How might mentors guide trainees' practice?
- How might mentors use questioning effectively to promote reflection and understanding?

SUMMARY

This chapter has provided a summary of the key policy changes which affect mentoring within the ITT context. Providers are responsible for shaping the roles of the lead mentor and for determining the content of ITAPs. Providers need to ensure that the minimum training requirements for mentors and for ITAP delivery are met. This chapter has summarised some key research that underpins the ITTECF.

CHECKLIST

- Mentors must have a deep understanding of the ITE curriculum.
- Mentors should also know the research evidence base which underpins the ITTECF.
- ITAPs should be designed to enable trainees to learn about pivotal and focused aspects of practice.

FURTHER READING

Department for Education (DfE) (2023) *Initial Teacher Training: Forming Partnerships. Updated Guidance.* [online] Available at: https://assets.publishing.service.gov.uk/media/64c7922619f562000df3c103/ITT_forming_partnerships_guidance_-_August_2023.pdf (accessed 28 March 2024).

This guidance provides information about the role of lead partners, teaching school hubs and other partnerships.

Schools Week (2024) New Teacher Training Framework: Everything You Need to Know. [online] Available at: https://schoolsweek.co.uk/dfe-combines-two-flagship-schemes-into-new-initial-teacher-training-and-early-career-framework-after-ecf-review (accessed 28 March 2024).

This blog provides a summary of the changes in the new ITTECF.

CHAPTER 2
PRINCIPLES, MODELS AND APPROACHES TO GENERIC MENTORING

CHAPTER OBJECTIVES

By the end of this chapter you will understand:

+ the characteristics of effective mentors;
+ the principles which underpin mentoring;
+ models and approaches to mentoring.

INTRODUCTION

Effective teachers draw on a range of pedagogical approaches from their pedagogical toolkits to enable them to carry out a variety of tasks. In the same way, mentors need a range of mentoring strategies in their mentoring toolkits to enable them to carry out their roles. Most teachers remember a great mentor, either from their ITT or from the early stages of their teaching careers. Mentors are required to support trainees and early career teachers (ECTs) but, at the same time, they also need to develop them by ensuring that there is an appropriate amount of challenge. This chapter explores the attributes of effective mentors, the principles that underpin effective mentoring, and approaches and models of mentoring.

EFFECTIVE MENTORING

Effective mentors establish positive relationships with their mentees (Izadinia, 2016; Ellis et al, 2020). They work collaboratively with their mentees and view mentoring as an opportunity to support their own professional growth as well as the professional growth of their mentees (Trevethan, 2017; Aderibigbe et al, 2018). They provide constructive feedback, listen to their mentees (Jones et al, 2021) and establish non-hierarchical relationships so that trainees can thrive (Mackie, 2020). However, these attributes can sometimes be difficult to maintain, especially when mentors are required to engage in critical dialogues with their trainees (Chan, 2020; Fletcher et al, 2021).

Power imbalances become evident when mentors switch from developing trainees to assessing them and making judgements on their professional competency (Mackie, 2020; Jones et al, 2021). A collaborative relationship between the mentor and trainee is usually beneficial (Donaldson, 2010; Aderibigbe et al, 2018; Jones et al, 2021). Effective mentors are knowledgeable and can model specific pedagogical approaches and provide valuable guidance on a range of matters (Nguyen and Hudson, 2012; Izadinia, 2016; Mena et al, 2017; Ellis et al, 2020). As well as carrying out more formal lesson observations, effective mentors also use incidental conversations as opportunities to develop trainees (Jones et al, 2019). They adopt a dialogic and democratic approach (Jones et al, 2021) to their mentoring.

PRINCIPLES OF MENTORING

Successful mentoring is dependent on trust, openness and mutual respect. Where relationships are strong, trainees and mentors can learn from each other. Pastoral care for mentees should be at the heart of all mentoring relationships. Mentors should acknowledge that trainees are individuals and have different needs and starting points. Effective mentors identify trainees' current stages of development and provide support to enable them to reach more advanced stages of development. Scaffolding therefore plays a critical role in advancing trainees' development. Mentors initially provide higher levels of support but gradually remove this as trainees become increasingly competent, so that eventually trainees can perform tasks independently. Mentors and mentees must establish appropriate professional boundaries from the outset. Effective mentors are sensitive and supportive but able to ensure that trainees are appropriately challenged.

COACHING AND MENTORING

Mentoring and coaching are not interchangeable terms. However, this chapter uses the terms coaching and mentoring interchangeably because the technique of coaching is being utilised by school-based mentors within the context of ITE. *Mentoring* is generally used within the context of an expert–novice relationship. Within this relationship, the mentor has knowledge and expertise, and the trainee or teacher can learn from that. Coaches do not necessarily identify as experts, but they have expertise that they can share which can help other colleagues to develop professionally. Coaching tends to use less directive approaches than mentoring. Skilled coaches ask questions, encourage colleagues to reflect on their own practice, and support colleagues to identify goals and actions.

FACILITATIVE APPROACHES

A 'one-size-fits-all' model for mentoring in teacher education does not exist (Parker et al, 2021). Effective mentors need a variety of approaches to meet the needs of different mentees.

A facilitative approach works on the principle that the trainee/teacher is knowledgeable, and they know what they need to do to improve. The coach generally offers support and encouragement, but they tend to adopt a 'hands-off' approach. They are a knowledgeable 'sounding board' rather than someone who gives advice. The coach does not share their expertise, and the teacher/trainee thinks through the problems and generates solutions for themselves. This approach is more aligned to coaching than mentoring.

DIRECTIVE APPROACHES

A directive approach to mentoring typically assumes that the teacher or trainee needs to be told what to do, that is, they are a novice. This is a 'master and apprentice' model. The role of the mentor is to share all their knowledge with the novice because they are the expert. Within this model, the mentor does most of the thinking. This approach is more akin to mentoring.

DIALOGICAL APPROACHES

Within a dialogical model, the trainee/teacher works in partnership with the coach/mentor, who is not necessarily an 'expert' but they have expertise which they want to share. Instructional coaching fits into this category. Within this model, both parties meet regularly and think through the problem together. Dialogical approaches are more akin to coaching than mentoring, and instructional coaching is one example of a dialogic approach. Dialogic coaching fits between facilitative and directive approaches.

INSTRUCTIONAL COACHING

Instructional coaching is an example of a dialogic approach. The use of coaching in teacher development has been evolving for several decades (Lofthouse, 2018). Within instructional coaching, both the mentor (or coach) and the trainee teacher contribute equally to the discussion (Knight, 2007). Knight's model of instructional coaching has three stages:

1. *Identify. The coach uses questioning with the teacher to promote reflection. Through this process, the coach and teacher identify a goal which will improve their teaching.*
2. *Learn. The coach uses a variety of mentoring approaches, including modelling, co-teaching, observation and feedback to support the teacher's development. The coach and teacher may view digital recordings of the teacher's lessons to facilitate critical evaluation. Throughout this stage, there is an emphasis on working together to facilitate teacher development.*
3. *Improve. The teacher implements the new strategies on their own and works with the coach to monitor their practice.*

(Knight, 2017)

Within this model, the relationship between the teacher and the coach is supportive. The coach encourages the teacher to identify the positive aspects in their practice. Once the goal has been achieved, the coach and the teacher repeat the cycle.

The cycle is represented in Figure 2.1 opposite. The relationship between the coach and teacher is built on trust. The assumption is

CHAPTER 2: PRINCIPLES, MODELS AND APPROACHES TO GENERIC MENTORING

that both parties can benefit from the relationship and that the coach and teacher can learn from each other. Scaffolding is a critical part of the model, particularly at Stage 2. The coach must engage in active listening and provide specific feedback about the teacher's progress towards achieving the identified goal. The model can support whole school improvement for teachers and pupils (Woolfolk Hoy and Spero, 2005; Marzano and Simms, 2014). Honesty and reflection are key components of this model.

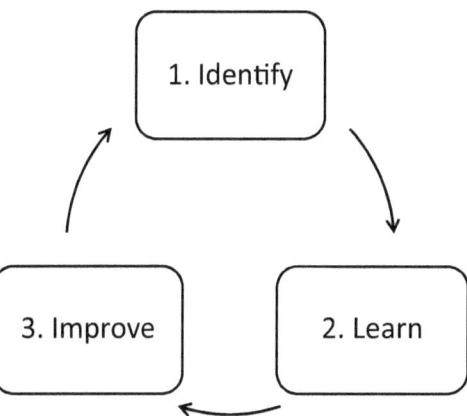

Figure 2.1 Adaptation of Knight's model of instructional coaching

Instructional coaches generally revisit the same skills several times so that teachers can practise them to automaticity.

Instructional coaching is also very different to what we might call business coaching, in which the coach asks a series of open questions to draw out the answers that people already, in some sense, know deep down. Instructional coaches are more directive, very intentionally laying a trail of breadcrumbs to move the novice from where they are currently, to where the expert wants them to be.

(Sims, 2019)

Alternative models of instructional coaching may include a rubric which specifies the skills that need to be mastered, and other models may also specify the techniques that the teacher needs to learn. Once a goal has been identified, the coach can help the teacher to break this down into smaller goals or milestones. The role of the coach is to set precise goals and then design mentoring/coaching approaches to enable the teacher to demonstrate these goals. The approach uses *deliberate practice*. Instructional coaching assumes that the coach is an expert in the specific areas of practice that need to be improved and that the teacher is a novice in these areas. This is why the model is effective in the context of ITE where trainee teachers are generally novices and the mentors are more experienced. Identified areas for improvement are very precise. For example, within an instructional coaching model it is not appropriate to set a vague target such as *'you need to improve your use of assessment'*. This is not a helpful target. The target might be better framed in the following ways:

+ Plan to use a hinge question in the lesson to check that pupils have understood the content.
+ After you have modelled the subject content to pupils in the lesson (*'I do'*), immediately introduce a *'we do'* task to provide the pupils with an opportunity to tell you about the steps through the problem. This allows the pupils to demonstrate to you that they have understood before you set them an independent task.

Within instructional coaching, coaches might:

+ identify, and clearly describe, the target performance (goal) that needs to be demonstrated: trainees and teachers need to know precisely what they need to change;
+ break this down into small components which can be practised;
+ design mentoring/coaching approaches to support the teacher/ trainee – for example, the coach might use modelling of specific pedagogical approaches;
+ practise the approaches in controlled conditions (for example, practise the skill with the coach/mentor before the teacher uses it for real);
+ provide feedback using open questioning and supported reflection – feedback is specific, detailed and focused on a narrow area of practice;
+ provide opportunities for the trainee/teacher to gradually work with increasing independence to allow them to master the goal.

Within instructional coaching there should be regular reflective meetings to discuss the desired outcome(s) and repeated, deliberate practice which enable trainees or teachers to master the techniques. Coaching sessions are usually conducted as one-to-one sessions. The process is intensive, and coaches/mentors and trainees/teachers meet regularly to review teacher development. The coaching generally takes place over an extended period of time, and the trainee/teacher focuses their attention on the acquisition of specific skills in their own practice.

DELIBERATE PRACTICE

In deliberate practice, the trainee practises a focused and clearly defined skill that has been identified. They then repeatedly focus their attention on this aspect of their practice to develop automaticity. Finally, they receive focused, high-quality feedback.

USING INSTRUCTIONAL COACHING IN ITT

Tom Sherrington's website offers some useful ideas. He states:

I'd willingly concede that most of the top-down fly-by feedback I've given over the years has been ignored or wrong with no impact on teaching quality. Because I was giving it – not helping the teacher to generate it; imposing my agenda, not helping the teacher with theirs.

(Sherrington, 2020)

Sherrington states that feedback delivered via a feedback sheet, or feedback that is logged onto an electronic portal, is not always effective because the receiver still has to hear the feedback, accept it and then act on it. Sherrington argues that teacher improvement is driven by teachers, that is, teachers can only improve themselves if they want to improve. He argues that identifying goals should be teacher driven, but this process can be supported by someone with experience and knowledge to share. Sherrington states that lesson feedback should be dialogic and supported by professional development which includes iterative cycles of reflection, planning and deliberate practice. Instructional coaching requires teachers/trainees and coaches to work together to identify goals and solutions. It requires multiple interactions over time and is a significant shift from one-off lesson drop-ins. The focus of the identified area of improvement is tight rather than trying to address multiple targets. Within this model, Sherrington advises that lesson observations should not be set up for the purpose of determining quality but should help teachers to self-identify what they need to improve.

CRITICAL QUESTIONS

+ Do you agree with Sherrington? Explain your answer.
+ What are the advantages of teacher-driven professional development?

VIDEO-BASED COACHING

Video-based instructional coaching involves filming a lesson delivered by a trainee or teacher. The coach might focus on a segment of the video, which is then discussed. The coach might play the video and pause it in specific places. They may ask questions about the part of the lesson which has been paused, such as *why did you use that approach? Did that approach work as well as you anticipated? What impact did it have on the pupils? What might you improve next time?*

CRITICAL QUESTIONS

+ What are the advantages and disadvantages of recording lessons?
+ What are the characteristics of effective questioning when reviewing recorded lessons?

USING COUNTING

Counting can be an effective strategy to promote reflection. The strategy works well when the trainee/teacher is asked to review a lesson they have taught which has been filmed or they might be asked to review the coach's transcript. Examples of questions which coaches might use in this strategy include the following:

+ How many pupils are engaged?
+ How many pupils are off task?
+ How long did the teacher input take?
+ How many times did you use this phrase ...?
+ How long did it take to get the lesson started?

- How many times did Oscar answer a question?
- How many times did you choose Archie to answer a question?

The nature of the questions will depend on the specific goal that the trainee/teacher is trying to achieve.

ENQUIRY-BASED OR COGNITIVE COACHING

Cognitive coaching uses questioning to support the trainee teacher to think about their practice. If a mentor wants a trainee to think more about timings in lessons when planning lessons, the coach might review the lesson plan with them and ask the following questions:

- How long do you anticipate that the introduction to the lesson will last?
- How long will it take to model the new subject content?
- How long do you expect the children will need to complete the task?

During a feedback session, the mentor might ask the following questions:

- How did you ensure the pupils all participated in the lesson?
- How did you ensure that the pupils remembered the key facts?
- How did you ensure that you had high ambition for pupils with special educational needs?
- What might you do differently?
- I noticed that Rhiannon and Abdul were off task. How could you have prevented this?
- I wonder what would have happened if you had done X rather than Y?
- What do you think could have been improved?
- Which aspects do you think went well?
- Which aspects did not go according to plan?

CRITICAL QUESTIONS

- Think of some more cognitive coaching questions.
- What do you notice about these types of questions?

BAMBRICK-SANTOYO'S SIX-STEP MODEL

Paul Bambrick-Santoyo (2012) sets out six aspects of effective feedback. These are summarised below:

1. **Provide precise praise:** An example is '*I like the way you engaged Arthur by asking him to write a word on the board*'.
2. **Probe:** Ask probing questions which encourage reflection, such as: '*Why do you think these specific pupils struggled to complete the task?*'
3. **Identify problems and provide concrete action steps:** This is where the trainee/teacher identifies the problem and suggests concrete action steps.
4. **Practice:** According to Paul Bambrick-Santoyo, great teaching is learned through *doing*, not through discussion. The coach might *model* the solution so that the trainee and teacher are clear about what they need to *do* to improve.
5. **Plan ahead:** At this stage trainees/teachers actively record what they need to do next by making notes.
6. **Set timeline:** Together, the trainee/teacher and coach agree a timeline for implementing the changes.

CRITICAL QUESTIONS

+ What aspects of this model do you like?
+ If you re-developed this model, are there any aspects that you would change and, if so, why?

CONTENT-FOCUSED COACHING

Content-focused coaching is an example of instructional coaching. The coach/mentor focuses on *what* the trainee is teaching first, with an emphasis on their subject content knowledge (ie trainees' knowledge of the subject matter). This naturally leads on to discussing pedagogical content knowledge (ie *how* to teach the content).

CASE STUDY

HISTORY: CONTENT COACHING

A trainee is teaching a primary-aged class about the Great Fire of London. The trainee has produced a lesson plan which outlines all the key facts that they are going to present to the pupils in the lesson. This includes the year when the fire broke out, how it started, how quickly the fire spread and an account of how the fire was extinguished.

The mentor is interested in exploring with the trainee how they intend to develop pupils' disciplinary knowledge in the lesson. The trainee understands the content that they are teaching but has not fully understood what is meant by disciplinary knowledge. The mentor advises the trainee to read the Ofsted research review for history (www.gov.uk/government/collections/curriculum-research-reviews).

In a subsequent mentoring session, the mentor asks the trainee for an update on their learning from reading this report. The trainee accurately states that disciplinary knowledge in history relates to the knowledge of how historians have studied specific aspects of the past and constructed claims and accounts about them. The mentor then asks the trainee how they might develop the pupils' knowledge of how historians studied the Great Fire of London. The trainee suggests that the pupils could look at Samuel Pepys' diary to find out more about the Great Fire of London.

RESEARCH-LED COACHING

In research-led coaching, mentors emphasise to trainees the underpinning research evidence that supports specific pedagogical approaches in the classroom. They will connect trainees' learning in school with the research studies that trainees have been introduced to during their centre-based training.

CRITICAL QUESTIONS

+ Which of the above approaches do you like?
+ Will you use one of the above approaches or will you draw on different approaches to coaching and mentoring? Explain your answer.

OBSERVATION

During lesson visits, mentors observe trainees in the classroom and provide them with constructive feedback. The problem with this approach is that mentors can focus on too many things, thus resulting in cognitive load for trainees. It is more effective to agree on a specific focus that the trainee is addressing in their practice rather than conducting a general observation of a lesson and commenting on everything that you have seen.

DECONSTRUCTION

Mentors might use deconstruction to isolate specific pedagogical approaches to students. This is sometimes known as deconstruction. Following a lesson visit, a mentor might say:

Did you notice when the teacher asked this specific question? [How many vertices does a square have?] This is called a **hinge question**. *This enabled the teacher to gauge whether the pupils had understood the declarative knowledge in mathematics. How did the teacher quickly ascertain the understanding of the whole class? What did the teacher do next following the response from the pupils?*

Mentors might use deconstruction to focus trainees' attention on specific aspects of pedagogy. In the above example, the mentor is focusing the trainee on questioning and assessment. A hinge question enables the teacher to quickly ascertain if pupils have understood the subject content. Hinge questions are generally asked to a whole class of pupils. If the pupils have understood the subject content, the teacher can progress to the next part of the lesson. If the pupils have not understood, the teacher may re-teach the content, address the misconceptions or ask the pupils who have understood to explain the content to the class.

CASE STUDY

DECONSTRUCTION

A mentor conducts a lesson visit with a trainee. The teacher is particularly skilled in managing low-level disruption during the lesson. Prior to the lesson visit, the mentor asks the trainee to note down all the strategies that the teacher uses during the lesson to manage low-level disruption.

During the subsequent mentoring session, the mentor gives the trainee some sticky notes and asks them to write all the strategies onto these – one strategy per sticky note. The mentor then asks the trainee to sort the sticky notes into two piles: verbal and non-verbal strategies. The mentor then asks the trainee to pick out two strategies that they will use in their next lesson and to explain the reasons for their selection.

GUIDED REFLECTION

Guided reflection uses effective questioning to focus trainees on specific aspects of their teaching. It is an approach which avoids telling trainees what they need to improve. Instead, the questions are carefully designed to support trainees to reflect deeply and critically on their own practice, thus guiding them towards self-identifying what they need to improve and what they are effective at.

RESEARCH

Research has highlighted that the expertise of the coach is a key factor in developing teachers (Blazar and Kraft, 2015). There is also some evidence that more effective coaches may also be more effective teachers (Goldhaber et al, 2020; Blazar et al, 2022).

SUMMARY

This chapter has outlined some of the characteristics of effective mentoring and the principles which underpin it. We have argued that coaching can play an important role within ITE mentoring and we have emphasised that effective mentors try to minimise power differentials between coaches and mentors.

CHECKLIST

+ One model of coaching may not be appropriate. Effective coaches and mentors might need to draw on different approaches to suit different circumstances at different times.
+ The relationship between the mentor and trainee is critical.
+ Effective mentoring relationships are based on trust, openness and honesty.
+ There are a range of different instructional coaching approaches.

FURTHER READING

Deans for Impact (2016) *Practice with Purpose: The Emerging Science of Teacher Expertise*. [online] Available at: https://deansforimpact.org/wp-content/uploads/2016/12/Practice-with-Purpose_FOR-PRINT_113016.pdf (accessed 28 March 2024).

Sims, S (2019) Four Reasons Instructional Coaching Is Currently the Best-Evidenced Form of CPD. *Sam Sims Quantitative Education Research*. [online] Available at: https://samsims.education/2019/02/19/247 (accessed 28 March 2024).

CHAPTER 3
THE ITE CURRICULUM AND IMPLICATIONS FOR MENTORS

> **CHAPTER OBJECTIVES**
>
> **By the end of this chapter you will understand:**
> + how to design the school-based component of the ITE curriculum;
> + approaches to mentoring which support the implementation of the ITE curriculum in schools.

INTRODUCTION

The ITE curriculum includes the content that is implemented in the centre and the content that is implemented by mentors in schools. The centre-based curriculum is typically delivered by the ITE provider in a range of settings, including universities. A well-designed ITE curriculum should enable trainee teachers to know more, remember more and do more. Trainees make progress by learning the content of the curriculum. It is only in recent years, following the implementation of the initial teacher education (ITE) inspection framework (Ofsted, 2024), that ITE providers have been required to design, with their partnerships, a well-sequenced curriculum which specifies the components that will be learned both in the centre and in schools. The components of the ITE curriculum which are implemented in schools should build on the content that has been delivered in the centre and/or provide trainees with opportunities to learn how to implement specific pedagogical approaches. The ITE curriculum must be designed to address all the statements that are set out in the Initial Teacher Training and Early Career Framework (DfE, 2024a) and provide opportunities for trainees to revisit and deepen their knowledge. This chapter outlines some considerations for mentors when implementing the ITE curriculum in schools.

THE INITIAL TEACHER TRAINING AND EARLY CAREER FRAMEWORK

The Initial Teacher Training and Early Career Framework (ITTECF) (DfE, 2024a) sets out the minimum content that trainee and early career teachers (ECTs) need to learn. It is not a curriculum because it does not break the composite knowledge down into smaller components of knowledge and it does not sequence content in a specific order. ITT providers, in partnership with their schools, are responsible for identifying the components of knowledge that trainees need to learn and for sequencing these components of knowledge to enable trainee teachers to know more, remember more and do more as they progress through the curriculum.

The content is divided into '*Learn that*' and '*Learn how to*' statements. Trainees can learn content from each of these strands through the centre-based ITT curriculum and the school-based ITT curriculum. It is a misconception that all the '*Learn how to*' statements must be learned in schools and that all the '*Learn that*' statements must be learned through the curriculum that is taught in the centre. Both centre- and school-based contexts provide opportunities for trainees to learn content knowledge and to develop their skills through application.

The latest version of the framework (DfE, 2024a) is listed in the References section at the end of the book. The content is the same, regardless of whether the teacher is a trainee teacher or an ECT. This is deliberately intended so that content which has been learned in ITT can be revised, built upon and contextualised to the schools or settings in which ECTs work.

Through the process of curriculum design, ITT providers, in partnership with their schools and lead mentors, are responsible for designing a well-sequenced ITT curriculum which provides opportunities for trainee teachers to revisit knowledge and deepen their knowledge. ITT partnerships are also responsible for identifying which aspects of the ITTECF will be learned through the centre-based curriculum and which aspects will be learned through the ITT curriculum in schools. The ITT curriculum includes both components of the curriculum: the centre-based component and the school-based component. The centre-based component is usually delivered by trainers, consultants, lecturers or tutors, but ITT providers can also involve expert mentors from schools in delivering specific components of the centre-based curriculum. The school-based component of the ITT curriculum is usually delivered by school-based mentors, subject leaders in schools or lead mentors that work for the ITT provider.

It is the responsibility of the ITT provider to ensure that mentors who are supporting trainees in schools know what trainees have learned (or are learning) in the centre-based curriculum. If mentors do not know what trainees have learned (or are learning) in the centre, the curriculum lacks coherence and mentors are not able to build effectively on trainees' knowledge. The following sections outline key elements from the ITTECF that trainees need to learn through the ITE curriculum in school. ITE partnerships will identify the elements of the ITTECF that will be learned through the curriculum in the centre and the curriculum in schools. Mentors can also use the ITTECF to guide them in their day-to-day work with trainees. This can be a useful document to refer to when providing trainees with feedback and when setting targets. The '*Learn how to*' strand of the Framework is particularly pertinent when planning training experiences in school, but it is also important to remember that trainees can also master content from the '*Learn that*' strand during their time in schools. This section does not address all the ITTECF statements because mentors can refer to the Framework for further information.

HIGH EXPECTATIONS

The ITTECF (DfE, 2024a) outlines the content that must be covered in this strand, and it is for ITE providers and their partnerships to decide which components will be covered both in the centre and in schools. Trainees must learn about the impact of disadvantage on attainment and the impact of home life on pupils' readiness to learn. It is critical that trainees understand the positive impact of high-quality teaching on life chances, particularly for disadvantaged pupils. Through the centre-based curriculum, ITE providers typically introduce trainees to pertinent research which explores the complexity of disadvantage, including specific population groups that were more likely to experience poverty.

Through the ITE curriculum which is implemented in schools, trainees need to learn how to promote challenge and demonstrate high aspirations through designing an ambitious curriculum for all pupils. They need to learn how to promote intentional and consistent language in their classrooms and how to create a culture of inclusion, for example, by modelling courteous behaviour. Through coaching, skilled mentors can support trainees to achieve appropriate noise levels in their classrooms which are conducive to learning. Mentors can teach trainees about the strategies that they can use in classrooms to elicit pupil participation. Mentors can also guide trainees to support them in achieving high levels of pupil concentration in lessons.

HOW PUPILS LEARN

Through the curriculum in the centre, it is likely that trainees will have been introduced to the role of memory in the learning process. Trainees should understand the role of working memory and long-term memory, recognising the importance of purposeful practice and retrieval. It is likely that they will have been introduced to cognitive load. They should know that pupils have different working memory capacities.

It is through the ITE curriculum in schools that trainees can start to apply this knowledge. Mentors can support trainees to plan lesson sequences to ensure that foundational knowledge is secure before introducing new subject content. Mentors can model to trainees how to break subject content down into smaller components to reduce cognitive load across a sequence of lessons. Mentors can create opportunities for trainees to observe teaching across the school. Observing lessons with trainees enables mentors to isolate specific aspects of practice in lessons. For example, mentors can support trainees to learn about the importance of explicit, direct teaching of subject content using the technique of exposition. Mentors can support trainees to learn about exposition through observing several lessons so that trainees start to understand that teachers can use a variety of approaches for exposition.

Through the ITE curriculum in schools, mentors can observe a variety of lessons with trainees to help them to understand the use of exposition, repetition, guided and independent practice, and retrieval in lessons. Mentors can subsequently, through a coaching session, support trainees to connect these approaches with the centre-based curriculum. To facilitate this, mentors could use the following critical questions to frame the discussion.

CRITICAL QUESTIONS

+ How did the teacher connect the new subject content to content previously learned?
+ How did the teacher reduce cognitive load during the exposition phase of the lesson?
+ What was the role of repetition and retrieval in this lesson?
+ What was the balance of retrieval, exposition, repetition and practice in this lesson?
+ When the teacher removed the scaffolding (fading), what did you notice about the level of challenge for pupils?

Mentors can support trainees with planning lessons to incorporate retrieval, exposition, repetition, and guided and independent practice. They can support trainees to plan for repetition, so the pupils develop fluency with the subject content.

SUBJECT KNOWLEDGE

Through the ITE curriculum in the centre, it is likely that trainees will have learned about the essential concepts, knowledge, principles and skills associated with the subject(s) that they are teaching. They are likely to have been introduced to the national curriculum goals for those subjects and they should be able to identify subject-specific misconceptions that pupils are likely to develop. The curriculum in the centre should typically have introduced trainees to different types of subject knowledge.

+ Substantive knowledge relates to the knowledge of the subject. This includes subject-specific principles, concepts, facts and skills.
+ Disciplinary knowledge relates to the knowledge of how subject experts work within a subject. For example, a historian does not just learn historical facts (substantive knowledge); they must also critically evaluate historical evidence and, on the basis of this, formulate reasoned opinions about life in the past. This is called disciplinary knowledge.

Through the ITE curriculum in schools, mentors can support trainees to learn how to plan lessons which address both types of subject knowledge. Trainees may focus on planning lessons to develop pupils' substantive knowledge in a subject, but if they are not focusing in their lesson planning on developing pupils' disciplinary knowledge, pupils will not learn enough about how to work within the subject. Through guided lesson planning, mentors in school can support trainees to identify and explicitly teach correct subject-specific vocabulary. They can help trainees to plan effective questions which develop pupils' thinking and enable them to check pupils' understanding. In addition, mentors can support trainees to develop their familiarity with published schemes or textbooks that are used in specific subjects.

Through guided visits of lessons, mentors can support trainees to recognise how teachers use demonstrations, examples, analogies and concrete resources to explain complex ideas and concepts. Mentors can support trainees to understand how teachers develop pupils' fluency with subject content, for example using repetition. Through guided visits of teaching, mentors can also support trainees to understand how teachers use summarising as a technique during lessons. Focusing on all these aspects within a single lesson is unlikely to be beneficial because it will result in cognitive load for the trainees. It is more effective if mentors support trainees to isolate one aspect of practice in a guided lesson visit.

CLASSROOM PRACTICE

Through the centre-based ITT curriculum, trainees will typically have learned about key pedagogical approaches, including modelling, scaffolding, fading, questioning and metacognitive strategies. Through the ITT curriculum in schools, trainees need to observe these approaches in lessons, plan to use them in their own teaching and reflect on their own development. Skilled mentors support trainees to plan lessons, linking new learning to prior learning. They can support trainees to plan homework tasks. Through guided lesson visits and supported lesson planning, they support trainees to develop their skills in breaking content and activities down into smaller parts, using visual and concrete representations in their teaching and designing effective questions to use in lessons. Through guided lesson visits, expert mentors can isolate specific strategies that teachers use in lessons, including modelling, explanations, scaffolding, fading and purposeful practice. A useful focus for a guided lesson visit is to look at how different grouping arrangements are used by different teachers or across different subjects. Mentors can support trainees to think critically about different grouping arrangements and to connect this with research on ability grouping and mixed-ability grouping.

CASE STUDY

METACOGNITIVE THINKING: GUIDED LESSON VISIT

A mentor undertakes a guided lesson visit with a trainee. The lesson focuses on writing in a Key Stage 2 class. The children are learning about how to write powerful descriptions of story settings. The teacher starts the lesson by thinking aloud some ideas to get the writing started. The teacher says the first sentence aloud and then starts to write it on the board: '*It was a cold night and the forest was dark*'. The teacher then re-reads the sentence aloud. The teacher then says aloud, but to herself: '*I need a more powerful adjective to describe the night. I think I'll use* bitter'. The pupils agree that this is a better adjective because it gives a better sense of how cold it is. The teacher then edits the sentence by replacing '*cold*' with '*bitter*'. The teacher then thinks aloud the next sentence and continues to edit the work. After the teacher has written the first three sentences, she then asks the pupils to work in pairs to think of the next sentence. The pupils use whiteboards to write the next sentence in pairs. The teacher then asks some of the pupils to share their ideas with the rest of the class. The teacher chooses one of the sentences and adds it to the shared text on the board. She asks the pupils if they can edit it to make the writing more vivid. This process continues. Following this input, the pupils then write their own story settings.

Following this lesson visit, the mentor coaches the trainee by asking some questions:

+ Did you notice how the teacher scaffolded the children's thinking through using metacognitive talk?
+ When was the teacher using modelling? Why was this part of the lesson important?
+ When was the teacher using scaffolding? What impact did this have on the pupils?
+ When did the teacher fade out the scaffolding? How did the teacher know this was the right time to remove the scaffolding?
+ When did the teacher use questioning to scaffold pupils' thinking? Why do you think they did this?

⟶

- Let's have a look at Rosenshine's principles of effective instruction that you have covered in your centre-based training. Which aspects were present in this lesson and which aspects did the teacher not use?
- How would you use metacognitive thinking in mathematics or science lessons? How might you use it in history or geography?

In this example, the mentor is skillfully supporting the trainee to isolate specific aspects of teaching so that these aspects are made very explicit to the trainee.

CRITICAL QUESTIONS

- In this case study, how did the mentor support the trainee to isolate specific pedagogical approaches?
- How did the mentor connect the ITT curriculum in schools to the ITT curriculum that was learned in the centre?

ADAPTIVE TEACHING

Through the curriculum in the centre, it is likely that trainees have been introduced to the Code of Practice for Special Educational Needs and/or Disabilities (SEND) (DfE and DoH, 2015), the underpinning principles of the Code, the concept of adaptive teaching and some key adaptive teaching strategies.

In the school-based ITT curriculum, trainees need to learn how to plan to meet the needs of all pupils in their lessons. One key aspect of the school component of the ITT curriculum is for the mentor to arrange a tutorial with the SENCO (Special Educational Needs Co-ordinator). The SENCO can support trainees to understand the school's SEND policy, how individual pupil needs are identified, the range of interventions that are available across the school for pupils with SEND and the characteristics of high-quality inclusive practice. The SENCO can plan a series of lesson visits which provide trainees with opportunities to observe the aspects of inclusive practice across the school. These might include the following:

- The entitlement for pupils with SEND to be in lessons with their peers.
- Pupils with SEND learning the same ambitious curriculum as their peers.

+ Pupils with SEND receiving access to specific adaptations during lessons.
+ Teachers demonstrating high expectations of all pupils.
+ Teachers using concrete and visual representations, examples, analogies and summarising in lessons.
+ Examples of scaffolding and fading in lessons.
+ Examples of collaborative work, for example paired work or group work.
+ Connecting new subject content to previous learning.
+ Use of repetition and retrieval.

Following the lesson visits, the SENCO can use coaching questions to help trainees to isolate the aspects of effective inclusive practice that they have seen.

Through the ITT curriculum in school, expert mentors can support trainees to understand the implementation of the graduated approach (DfE and DoH, 2015) within schools. Trainees can review education, health and care plans (EHCPs) for specific pupils and subsequently observe these pupils in lessons. Mentors can also arrange for trainees to 'shadow' interventions for pupils with SEND and meetings with parents, as well as understanding approaches for monitoring the impact of interventions. Trainees can look at records that are kept on specific pupils with SEND, including how behaviour incidents or specific concerns are documented and analysed. Expert mentors can arrange for trainees to 'shadow' external professionals, including speech and language therapists, educational psychologists and occupational therapists. If there is specialist SEND provision on site or locally, expert mentors can design further learning opportunities related to this. These aspects cannot be learned through the ITT curriculum in the centre.

CASE STUDY

SUPPORTING PUPILS WITH SEND: GUIDED PLANNING

A subject mentor supports a trainee to consider how to adapt a lesson for pupils with SEND. The trainee is teaching in Key Stage 3 and is a science specialist. There is a pupil in the class with dyslexia who finds

⟶

writing difficult. The pupil has short-term memory difficulties. They find it difficult to remember subject content that has previously been taught and they can only process a limited amount of new subject content in a single lesson. This session is a guided planning coaching session.

- The subject mentor starts the session by asking the trainee to identify the barriers to learning for this pupil.
- The mentor then asks the trainee to draw on their centre-based training to explain the concept of adaptive teaching. The trainee can explain how the concept of adaptive teaching differs from the concept of differentiation.
- The mentor then asks the trainee to identify some adaptive teaching strategies which might be useful. The trainee struggles to do this at first, so the mentor asks them to look at the notes from the training session that was taught in the centre. The mentor and the trainee review the training materials and they identify that, in this lesson, the pupil may benefit from the use of a pre-teach. It is not possible to withdraw the pupil from other lessons for a pre-teach, so the mentor suggests that the trainee produces a short five-minute video recording to explain the key subject-specific terminology and concepts. This is then made available to all students in advance of the lesson via the learning platform and is available for pupils to view.
- The mentor supports the trainee to think through the lesson structure, subject-specific vocabulary and concepts, as well as to integrate visual and concrete representation, examples and analogies to support pupils with their understanding of abstract subject content. The mentor supports the trainee to limit the subject content in the lesson.

CRITICAL QUESTIONS

- How does the mentor use coaching in this training session to scaffold the trainee's thinking?
- What might a follow-on coaching session entail?
- How is the mentor developing the trainee's understanding of high-quality inclusive teaching for all pupils?

ASSESSMENT

Through the ITE curriculum, which is delivered in the centre, it is likely that trainees will have been introduced to the purpose of assessment in schools, the characteristics of high-quality feedback and some pedagogical approaches for assessing pupils' knowledge. Trainees may also have been introduced to approaches for reducing their workload when marking pupils' work and providing them with feedback.

Through the ITE curriculum in school, it is important that trainees practise making assessment an integral part of their teaching. They should have opportunities to observe teachers using assessment and providing pupils with feedback within lessons. Mentors can support trainees to plan for assessment when designing lessons and lesson sequences. Initially, mentors might typically guide trainees in identifying the types of questions that might be used in their lessons to check pupils' understanding and to deepen pupils' thinking. One approach to questioning is the use of hinge questions in lessons to check pupils' understanding. Mentors can support trainees to design quizzes or tests to check pupils' knowledge and to design assessment tasks within lessons to identify whether pupils have retained and understood the knowledge. Trainees must have opportunities to practise providing pupils with feedback and to experiment with developing pupil self- and peer assessment within lessons.

Mentors can introduce trainees to statutory assessment tests, including marking schemes and examination papers, and trainees might be given an opportunity to observe an assessment under controlled conditions. Mentors can engage trainees in marking examination papers and moderating pupils' work. They can also introduce trainees to the school policy on assessment, marking and feedback and to the data monitoring system that the school uses to capture internal assessment data. Expert mentors should allow trainees to participate in assessment activities, including in and between school moderation activities. Trainees should have opportunities to meet with the assessment leader to discuss the approaches to assessment, with a specific focus on how knowledge gaps in pupils are identified and addressed. Much of this content cannot be learned in the centre.

MANAGING BEHAVIOUR

Through the curriculum in the centre, it is likely that trainees will have been introduced to theories that underpin behaviour, theories of motivation (intrinsic and extrinsic) and theories of self-esteem.

Through the ITE curriculum in schools, trainees need to learn about the whole school policy for supporting and managing pupils' behaviour. Mentors should provide trainees with opportunities to observe a variety of teachers to identify how low-level disruption is managed in classrooms. In addition, through guided lesson visits, mentors can support trainees to understand how relationships, routines and responses influence behaviour. In school, trainees need to learn about the school policy for sanctions and rewards, and mentors can support trainees through guided coaching to use agreed language and agreed non-verbal signals for addressing behaviour. Mentors, in partnership with ITE providers, are well placed to design a 'behaviour curriculum' for trainees. This is a curriculum which identifies each of the components of knowledge that trainees need to learn to effectively support and manage pupils' behaviour. This might include:

+ behaviour policy and systems;
+ using descriptive praise;
+ strategies for addressing low-level disruption;
+ non-verbal strategies;
+ managing transitions;
+ addressing defiance and other challenging behaviours;
+ addressing behaviour outside of classrooms;
+ responding to bullying;
+ learning routines;
+ behaviour and Special Educational Needs and/or Disabilities;
+ diffusing behaviours;
+ regulation;
+ working in partnership with parents;
+ behaviour and safeguarding.

This is not an exhaustive list of curriculum components, and it cannot all be taught at once. Mentors will need to decide how to sequence the components and design opportunities for trainees to practise each component to automaticity. This will enable them to become fluent in the implementation of aspects of the behaviour curriculum. Mentors can coach trainees in how to record incidents and how to communicate with parents. Mentors might explore case study examples which illustrate how teachers manage specific situations where behaviour is a focus. If there is a 'regulation room' in the school, mentors can arrange for trainees to meet with the member of staff who leads this provision to learn about the purpose of the room and the pedagogical approaches which are implemented in that space.

PROFESSIONAL BEHAVIOURS

Through the curriculum in the centre, trainees may have been introduced to the role of relevant subject associations, theories of reflective practice and the research which underpins the effective deployment of teaching assistants. All trainees will learn about safeguarding through the centre-based curriculum. The centre-based curriculum should have introduced trainees to relevant up-to-date educational research.

In schools, mentors should support trainees to understand and participate in the school's extra-curricular offer. Trainees should meet with the designated safeguarding lead to learn about the school safeguarding policy and in particular how to respond to safeguarding concerns and disclosures. The ITE provider typically ensures that trainees have undertaken an approved safeguarding assessment prior to going into schools; this may include a separate assessment which tests trainees' knowledge of the Prevent duty. Through guided coaching, mentors should support trainees to organise, prioritise and manage their workload. Mentors should also 'check in' on trainees regularly to ensure that there are no well-being concerns. Mentors may also wish to coach trainees on the theme of self-care and introduce them to strategies for managing workload. Trainees should have opportunities to meet with subject leaders and other key staff, including the SENCO and the designated senior lead for mental health. Mentors may design opportunities for trainees to 'shadow' meetings with parents and to observe SEND review meetings.

CRITICAL QUESTIONS

+ How can ITE providers quality assure the implementation of the ITE curriculum in schools?
+ What factors in school can affect the implementation of the ITE curriculum?

INTENSIVE TRAINING AND PRACTICE (ITAP)

Periods of Intensive Training and Practice (ITAP) provide trainees with an opportunity to learn about a very focused aspect of educational practice. Each ITAP focuses on specific, foundational or pivotal areas of the ITT curriculum and allows trainees to bridge the connection between educational research and classroom practice. Some aspects of the ITAP will take place in schools, and other components can be delivered through the ITT provider.

Integrating ITAPs into training is a new requirement for ITT providers in England from 2024. Undergraduate programmes must include 30 days of ITAPs and postgraduate programmes must include 20 days (DfE, 2024b).

ITAPs should be designed collaboratively between ITT providers and mentors. Typically, lead mentors will be involved in designing, delivering and quality assuring ITAP provision.

The focus areas of ITAP should:

+ *be pivotal or foundational concepts of the planned ITT curriculum that trainees can put into practice immediately;*
+ *be granular in nature; and*
+ *have potential to impact on trainees' classroom practice irrespective of context.*

(DfE, 2024b, p 23)

ITAPs typically include structured observation of selected teaching practice, through observation of either live or recorded lessons and critical analysis of observed teaching. Trainees should receive guided input from an expert who will typically support them in isolating aspects of pivotal practice from lessons they have observed. The expert will also support them in designing classroom activities which focus on the identified aspect(s) of pivotal practice which they will rehearse. Focused observation, live modelling by experts, live classroom teaching, theoretical input and focused feedback are key components of each ITAP.

DESIGNING AN AMBITIOUS CURRICULUM

ITT providers, with their partnerships, are required to design an ambitious curriculum which exceeds the minimum requirements of the ITTECF. This content might include aspects of education which are not included in the ITTECF, such as subject leadership in schools, trauma-informed practice or training, restorative approaches for supporting behaviour and race equality in schools.

THE ROLES AND RESPONSIBILITIES OF MENTORS

Mentors are responsible for implementing the ITE curriculum in school. In England all trainee teachers are entitled to 1.5 hours of mentoring each week. Mentors are responsible for providing opportunities for trainees to learn from observing live teaching, modelling practice, deconstructing aspects of practice with trainees, guiding trainees to reflect on their own practice and providing trainees with feedback.

LEAD MENTORS

ITE partnerships in England must identify lead mentors. Lead mentors are expert mentors who take greater responsibility for curriculum design and supervision of mentors across the ITE partnership. They may lead training of other mentors and take responsibility for quality assuring the mentoring across the ITE partnership. Normally, they will take a lead role in designing the ITAPs and supervising mentors who are implementing ITAPs in school.

CRITICAL QUESTIONS

+ What are the pivotal and foundational aspects of practice that might form the basis of an ITAP?
+ What might ITE providers need to consider when designing ITAPs?

RESEARCH

+ In the technique of *instructional coaching* mentors typically provide trainees with prescriptive guidance which specifies the skills and techniques that they need to master (Sims, 2019). Clear goals are usually identified for the trainee to achieve, along with strategies to enable trainees to achieve these.

+ Feiman-Nemser (1998) developed the term *educative mentoring* in the United States. The mentor acts as a critical friend, adopting a supportive approach to encourage the trainee to become autonomous. It is a less directive approach than instructional coaching. The mentor will typically 'think aloud' to support the student.

Mentors need to use a range of approaches, and instructional coaching can be used within the broad framework of an educative approach (White and Mackintosh, 2022).

SUMMARY

This chapter has outlined examples of components of the ITE curriculum which can be implemented in the centre and in schools. It has introduced the purpose of ITAPs and the role of lead mentors.

CHECKLIST

+ The ITE curriculum must be designed by ITE providers with their partnerships.
+ The ITTECF is not a curriculum. It is a framework.
+ The ITE curriculum is delivered and learned in the centre and in schools by mentors.
+ The ITE curriculum in schools should provide opportunities to deepen trainees' knowledge and opportunities to learn how to implement specific pedagogical approaches.

FURTHER READING

Sherrington, T and Caviglioli, O (2020) *Teaching Walkthrus: Five-Step Guides to Instructional Coaching*. Woodbridge: John Catt.

Stanulis, R N, Wexler, L J, Pylman, S, Guenther, A, Farver, S, Ward, A, Croel-Perrien, A and White, K (2019) Mentoring as More Than 'Cheerleading': Looking at Educative Mentoring Practices through Mentors' Eyes. *Journal of Teacher Education*, 70(5): 567–80.

CHAPTER 4
INCLUSIVE MENTORING

CHAPTER OBJECTIVES

By the end of this chapter you will understand:

+ the implications of the Equality Act 2010 for mentors;
+ approaches for supporting inclusive mentoring.

INTRODUCTION

This chapter provides practical guidance on approaches which facilitate inclusive approaches to mentoring within the ITT/ITE context. Inclusion should be a proactive rather than a reactive response. This means that it should be considered from the outset and planned for, rather than being addressed 'in the moment'. Trainees are more likely to thrive if they experience a sense of belonging. If their identities are valued and respected, this enables them to be authentic in the workplace. However, inclusion is rarely straightforward, and you may encounter challenges along the way. You may also get things wrong, unintentionally. We can learn from these experiences to grow professionally. You will sometimes encounter 'inclusion challenges' and not know the solutions. Working through issues with trainees in partnership is likely to be beneficial. You do not need to have all the solutions and you do not need to know everything about inclusion, but maintaining an open mind, being willing to listen and being reflective will go a long way towards addressing the thorny issues that inclusion may present.

EQUALITY ACT 2010

The Equality Act 2010 is the legislative framework which underpins your practice as a mentor. The Equality Act identifies nine protected characteristics. This chapter does not address all of these but covers the ones which are likely to be more pertinent to trainees. The protected characteristics include age; disability; gender reassignment; marriage and civil partnership; pregnancy and maternity; race; religion or belief; sex; and sexual orientation. It is unlawful for ITE providers and schools to discriminate against individuals because of a protected characteristic. Discrimination can be either direct or indirect.

+ **Direct discrimination** occurs when a person is treated less favourably than another because they have a protected characteristic. It can also occur when individuals are treated less favourably because someone perceives that they have a protected characteristic or because the individual is connected to someone who has a protected characteristic. This final example is known as 'discrimination by association'.

+ **Indirect discrimination** occurs when there is a policy, arrangement or rule that applies in the same way for everybody but disadvantages a group of people who share a protected characteristic.

CRITICAL QUESTIONS

+ Can you think of any examples of direct discrimination?
+ Can you think of examples of indirect discrimination?

DISCRIMINATION TASKS

Consider each of the following scenarios and decide if they are examples of direct or indirect discrimination and state the reasons why in each case.

Table 4.1 Types of discrimination

Scenario	Direct	Indirect
A mature applicant for an ITE programme is informed that they have been unsuccessful because they are too old to be a teacher.		
A trainee with dyslexia makes a spelling mistake. The mentor criticises them and says that people with dyslexia should not be teachers.		
A trainee is socially transitioning from female to male. The school refuses to use he/him pronouns and insists that the pupils use the title 'Ms'.		
A trainee who is pregnant is told that they cannot sit down during lessons.		
A Jewish trainee is not allowed to leave early on Friday afternoons to engage in religious practices.		
A male trainee is asked to help the caretaker to lift some heavy equipment, but the female trainees are not required to do this.		
A staff dress code is introduced which requires women to wear skirts. There is a Muslim female trainee in the school.		
A pupil calls a male trainee 'gay'. The trainee reports it. The advice given is to ignore it; it is just 'banter'.		
A pupil makes a remark about terrorists in front of a Muslim trainee. The school doesn't want to draw attention to this, so they tell the trainee to ignore it.		

Now consider the following scenarios and decide what type of discrimination is being described.

Table 4.2 Further examples of discrimination

Scenario	Direct	Discrimination by perception	Discrimination by association
A pupil assumes that a trainee is a lesbian and makes an offensive comment about lesbians.			
A trainee has a disabled partner and needs to leave by 4.30pm to care for them. The trainee is told that they cannot leave school at that time, but other staff members leave at 4pm.			
A teacher in the staffroom makes a casual joke about two same-sex parents.			
A mentor consistently misgenders a trainee who is non-binary.			
A male trainee is criticised for not handing their planning in on time. The mentor says that *'male trainees are always disorganised and need to be "spoon-fed"'*. A female trainee also does not hand her planning in and is not criticised.			
A trainee has a partner who is transitioning into a different gender. A teaching assistant makes some unkind comments about this to another colleague and the trainee overhears these.			

→

Table 4.2 (Continued)

Scenario	Direct	Discrimination by perception	Discrimination by association
A trainee with hearing impairment is told that she cannot teach phonics because of the way she enunciates the sounds of speech.			
A trainee with dyslexia is not allowed to teach English because they keep making spelling mistakes.			
A trainee with a physical disability is not allowed to teach physical education due to health and safety reasons.			
A trainee has chronic fatigue syndrome, which is diagnosed mid-way through their training. The trainee needs to do a part-time placement over a longer duration, to allow them to recuperate. The ITE provider informs the trainee that a part-time placement for a longer period of time is not possible.			

CRITICAL QUESTIONS

+ Are there any scenarios which you are unsure about? Explain why.
+ Can you think of other examples of discrimination by perception?
+ Can you think of other examples of discrimination by association?

UNDERSTANDING TRAINEES' NEEDS

The starting point for mentors is to understand the specific needs of trainees. Some trainees will have individual support plans which the ITE provider has developed. These can be shared with schools, with the trainee's permission. Trainees who receive disability funding should have a support plan which outlines their needs. In cases where trainees agree for these plans to be shared, it is helpful for mentors to meet with trainees prior to the start of a placement to discuss how the school can best meet their needs and to identify the adjustments that are needed. Many trainees with protected characteristics will not have individual support plans because they do not need additional provisions to be implemented.

Trainees do not have to disclose a protected characteristic. However, if they do disclose that they have a protected characteristic, it can make it easier for mentors to meet their needs. Trainees may be happy to make a disclosure if they feel that they will be supported and that the school is inclusive for pupils and staff. It can be useful to arrange a meeting with the trainee, mentor and representative from the ITE provider to discuss the trainee's needs before a placement starts, provided that the trainee agrees to this meeting taking place. This strategy can help the trainee to feel completely supported. The meeting will enable the various stakeholders to plan to appropriately address the trainee's protected characteristic(s).

SUPPORTING TRAINEES WITH DISABILITIES

Trainees with disabilities are legally protected from direct or indirect discrimination. ITE providers and mentors must make *reasonable adjustments* to ensure that disabled trainees have equality of opportunity. Mentors and ITE providers should not lower their standards for trainees with disabilities. This is particularly important because all trainees must be able to demonstrate that they meet the Teachers' Standards at the end of their training. However, mentors and ITE providers can put adjustments in place to enable trainees with disabilities to meet the same professional standards that all trainees are required to achieve.

CRITICAL QUESTIONS

+ Why is the term *reasonable adjustments* potentially problematic?
+ What do *reasonable adjustments* mean to you?

Mentors are generally skilled at adapting their teaching to meet the needs of pupils with specific needs. They might break a task down into smaller steps to make it more manageable. This strategy can also be used for trainees with disabilities. The nature of the reasonable adjustments will depend on the specific needs of the trainee.

Trainees with autism may benefit from focused coaching on how to receive critical feedback and how to establish social connections with other colleagues in school. Tasks which they are required to do, meetings that they need to attend and expected outputs should be clearly identified or scheduled at the start of placements. Trainees with dyslexia may benefit from a range of interventions, including coloured overlays to lay over text, electronic spellcheckers, alternative formats for lesson plans (organising plans as 'mind maps'), additional coaching for phonics, grammar, punctuation or spelling, and scaffolded opportunities to practise reading aloud in class. Trainees with visual impairment may benefit from the use of enlarged text and seating plans. Those with hearing impairment may need to use assistive technology, and trainees with physical disabilities might benefit from physical adaptations to the layout of a classroom to enable them to move around the room. Mentors will need to check that the school building and classrooms are accessible; if accessibility is a problem, adjustments will need to be implemented.

It is not appropriate to identify adaptations based on 'categories' of disability. Trainees have individual needs, and strategies that are effective for one person with a specific disability may not be effective for another person with the same disability. It is therefore critical that ITE providers and their partnership schools adopt a person-centred approach by involving trainees in planning for reasonable adjustments. It is also important to adopt a continual reflective approach during a placement, particularly if the adaptations that have been implemented are not effective.

Trainees with disabilities make a valuable contribution to the teaching profession. They also act as powerful role models for pupils with disabilities.

CHAPTER 4: INCLUSIVE MENTORING

RESEARCH

Jacobs et al (2021) investigated the placement experiences of trainee teachers with dyslexia. The researchers found that some mentors made them feel that they were unsuitable for teaching, thus illustrating the tensions which exist between inclusion and the ableist/performative discourse in teaching. They found that mentors focused on the difficulties that trainees experienced because of their dyslexia (for example, difficulties with aspects of literacy), rather than their strengths. This demonstrated that mentors tended to adopt a deficit view of dyslexia. The researchers found that trainees with dyslexia (and sometimes their mentors) were able to identify strengths in their teaching, including their use of creative pedagogies in lessons to engage pupils. The trainees were often frustrated during school placements because they could not access the support services provided by their ITE provider, due to lack of time and logistical issues. The research identified that mentor training and development in this area was not adequate.

CASE STUDY

TRAINEE WITH DYSLEXIA

Emily was diagnosed with dyslexia during her undergraduate degree while studying at university. She was now a trainee teacher working in a primary school. Emily struggled with key aspects of literacy, including phonics and spelling. Her mentor provided her with some videos of each of the different phonemes that she was required to teach. The videos did not show Emily how to teach the lesson, but they taught her how to enunciate the phonemes and put them into words for reading. Emily found the lesson plan template that she had been given difficult to follow. Her mentor gave her a lesson plan format which allowed her to create a mind map of the lesson content. Emily found this easier for her to use. The mentor also allowed Emily to audio record mentor meetings because she often forgot what had been discussed and the actions that she needed to implement. The school provided Emily with an electronic spellchecker which she could use in lessons to help her with spelling.

SUPPORTING TRAINEES WHO ARE PREGNANT

Trainees who are pregnant should be risk assessed by the school and the ITE provider to ensure that they are able to flourish during school placements. The risk assessment will identify the risks and it should state the mitigations that are in place to address the risks. Examples of adjustments might include:

+ frequent opportunities to sit down on an appropriate adult chair during lessons;
+ adequate breaks between teaching commitments;
+ time out of school to attend medical or other appointments related to the pregnancy, such as antenatal care;
+ space and time to rest;
+ access to cooled drinking water;
+ allowing trainees to eat snacks when needed;
+ access to fresh air and opportunities to move around;
+ alterations to the hours of work;
+ avoiding heavy lifting and working at heights.

CRITICAL QUESTIONS

+ Can you identify any risks to a trainee who is pregnant?
+ Can you identify any other adjustments to support a trainee who is pregnant?

SEX DISCRIMINATION

Sex is a protected characteristic in the Equality Act. This means that trainees should not be treated less favourably due to their sex. Examples of sex discrimination include the following:

+ Negative comments about a specific gender, such as comments which reflect a view that male trainees are less organised than female trainees or that male trainees need more support than female trainees.

- Different expectations for male and female trainees in relation to physical contact with children.
- Different expectations for male and female trainees in relation to any aspect of the teacher's role.
- Not providing separate toilets for male staff but providing toilets for female staff.

CRITICAL QUESTIONS

- Can you think of other examples of sex discrimination in schools?
- How do sexist viewpoints develop?

RESEARCH

Eldred et al (2022) investigated the experiences of a group of male trainee teachers. They found that male trainees were asked to leave the room when pupils were asked to change into their kits for physical education, even though female trainees were allowed to remain in the room while children were getting changed. The male trainees engaged in self-surveillance strategies to ensure that they were not vulnerable to false allegations. They deliberately distanced themselves from pupils and avoided physical contact with pupils. They felt that their gender made them more vulnerable to accusations than female trainees.

TRANS/TRANSGENDER TRAINEES

Gender reassignment (or transitioning) is a protected characteristic. It is important to be familiar with the following terminology, which is taken from the Stonewall website (nd):

- **Gender reassignment.** To undergo gender reassignment usually means to undergo some sort of medical intervention, but it can also mean changing names, pronouns, dressing differently and living in their self-identified gender. Therefore, gender reassignment can be either a medical or social process.

- **Non-binary.** A term for people whose gender identity does not align with 'man' or 'woman'.
- **Trans.** An umbrella term to describe people whose gender is not the same as, or does not sit comfortably with, the sex they were assigned at birth. This can include people who are transgender, but it also includes people who are non-binary or gender fluid.
- **Transgender man.** A term used to describe someone who is assigned female at birth but identifies and lives as a man. This may be shortened to trans man, or FTM, an abbreviation for female to male.
- **Transgender woman.** A term used to describe someone who is assigned male at birth but identifies and lives as a woman. This may be shortened to trans woman, or MTF, an abbreviation for male to female.
- **Transitioning.** The steps a trans person may take to live in the gender with which they identify. Each person's transition will involve different things. For some this involves medical intervention, such as hormone therapy and surgeries, but not all trans people want or are able to have this. Transitioning also might involve things such as telling friends and family, dressing differently and changing official documents.
- **Transphobia.** The fear or dislike of someone based on the fact they are trans, including denying their gender identity or refusing to accept it. Transphobia may be targeted at people who are, or who are perceived to be, trans.

Trainee teachers who are undergoing gender reassignment, either as a social process or via medical intervention, are protected by the Equality Act. If the trainees are happy to disclose this to the school (and they are not required to do so), the following steps can help to facilitate their inclusion:

- Talk to the trainee about the name and title they wish to be known by. Find out how they want the pupils to address them. Find out how they want other staff to address them.
- Ask them for their pronouns.
- Discuss which toilets the trainee wishes to use. They are allowed by law to use the toilets that align with their gender.
- Discuss the school dress code and if any adjustments need to be made.

- Ask them if they have any concerns or anxieties they wish to discuss.
- Reassure them that the school is committed to inclusion and will ensure that any cases of discrimination from staff, pupils or parents will be taken seriously.
- Discuss if they require time away from school to attend any appointments at health or well-being services.
- Tell them who to report their concerns to.
- Ask them if they require any further adjustments.

The trainee may be anxious because they may be expecting to be exposed to some forms of discrimination from parents, pupils and possibly staff. Although you cannot guarantee that they will not encounter discrimination, it is important to reassure them that any discrimination will be taken seriously, documented and addressed.

LESBIAN, GAY AND BISEXUAL TRAINEES

Lesbian, gay and bisexual trainees may also be worried that they will encounter discrimination in school. You should not discuss sexual orientation with trainees unless they raise it directly with you. However, it is important to reassure all trainees at the start of a placement that the school is committed to inclusion and that cases of discrimination will be treated seriously. It is important that all trainees know how to report any cases of discrimination. If the trainees openly disclose their sexual orientation, there may be staff members in school who are also LGBT+ and are willing to act as a pastoral mentor so that there is a point of contact to discuss any well-being issues.

The National Education Union (NEU) LGBT+ *Inclusion Charter* states the following:

- *All members of the school/college body should have the right to feel safe and protected.*
- *Everyone should feel empowered to be able to be open about their sexual orientation and/or their gender identity without fear of bullying, stigma or ridicule.*
- *Silence or stigma in relation to LGBT+ people is a form of inequality.*
- *Schools should actively encourage and promote the visibility of LGBT+ students and staff and develop a sense of pride in LGBT+ identities.*

+ Schools should place LGBT+ discrimination, bullying or name-calling on the same footing as racism, sexism and disablism.
+ Schools should report and record all incidents of LGBT+ phobic bullying and encourage a culture where reporting is seen as important in creating the right climate.
+ Schools should commit to challenging sexism and gender stereotypes across the curriculum and to tackle outdated ideas about men's and women's abilities and achievements, understanding that sexist and homophobic ideas and opinions reinforce each other.

(NEU, 2023)

CRITICAL QUESTIONS

+ Why might LGBT+ trainees be reluctant to disclose their sexual orientation or gender identity?
+ Should LGBT+ trainees take a lead role in developing an LGBT+ curriculum for pupils?
+ How might you respond if a pupil makes a homophobic, lesbophobic, biophobic or transphobic comment to a trainee?

CASE STUDY

LGBT+ INCLUSION

Jordan was a gay trainee. He was open about his sexual orientation from the outset. The school had created a staff LGBT+ network. It was a large secondary school. The school invited Jordan to participate in the staff network and Jordan was happy to do so. The group were in the process of writing the LGBT+ inclusion policy. Jordan was able to contribute to the development of the policy. He took responsibility for researching ways of integrating LGBT+ content into the curriculum for different subjects. After two weeks, Jordan shared his research with the network and his suggestions were incorporated into the policy. The network organised an event for LGBT+ history month and Jordan participated in this.

RACE AND RACISM

Race includes colour, nationality and ethnic or national origins. Race also covers ethnic and racial groups. This means a collective of people who all share the same protected characteristic of ethnicity or race. Racism is a structural barrier perpetuated by individuals against a person because of their race. Treating trainees less favourably than another colleague on grounds of race, colour, nationality, or ethnic or national origins is direct race discrimination.

Mentors should discuss the race equality policy with all trainees. It is important that trainees feel that they can express their concerns and know how to report racism if it occurs. Trainees' well-being is a priority, particularly if the trainee is the only person of colour in the school. Mentors should regularly 'check in' with trainees to temperature-test their well-being. Schools can benefit enormously by having a diverse mix of staff. Schools should therefore consider the benefits that diverse representation can bring to the school community. Examples of racism may include:

+ failing a trainee without adequate support being implemented;
+ not allowing the trainee to enter the staffroom for social breaks;
+ moving away from a trainee (micro-aggression);
+ criticising the trainee's teaching repeatedly and not providing adequate support.

Research shows that Global Majority teachers:

+ *work within a predominantly white profession, even in urban schools serving diverse communities;*
+ *are concentrated in London schools and in ethnically diverse schools;*
+ *tend to work in disadvantaged schools, particularly in London;*
+ *are open and motivated to teach in urban diverse schools;*
+ *experience fewer opportunities for career progression.*

(Tereshchenko et al, 2020)

RELIGION

The Equality Act defines *religion* as being any religion, and *belief* as any religious or philosophical belief. A lack of religion or a lack of belief are also protected characteristics. Mentors should consider whether it is possible to provide trainees with prayer breaks during the day. It is not a requirement for schools to provide this, but proper consideration of the request should be given, considering the impact on the trainee, the impact on colleagues and the impact on the school. In addition, mentors are not required by law to approve time off for the trainee to attend religious celebrations, but they should consider the request carefully and comply with the policy of the ITE provider. Mentors should review the staff dress policy to ensure that it does not result in indirect discrimination for trainees with particular religious or other beliefs.

AGE

Mentors should ensure that trainees are not treated less favourably because of their age. Not allowing trainees to undertake particular activities because they are perceived to be too young or too old would constitute age discrimination if other trainees are allowed to participate in those activities.

SUMMARY

This chapter is a starting point for considering effective inclusion of trainees with protected characteristics. It does not provide a comprehensive toolkit of approaches because some of the 'detail' which underpins inclusive approaches will need to be tailored to meet the specific needs of students.

CHECKLIST

+ Trainees with one or more protected characteristics are protected by the Equality Act 2010.
+ Schools should have policies in place to promote equality. The onus should not be on the trainee to suggest ways forward to facilitate inclusion.
+ Discrimination can be direct or indirect.

FURTHER READING

National Education Union (NEU) (2022) School-Based Teacher Training: Your Rights and Expectations. [online] Available at: https://neu.org.uk/latest/library/school-based-teacher-training-your-rights-and-expectations (accessed 28 March 2024).

This guidance provides useful advice on the rights of trainee teachers.

Office for Standards in Education, Children's Services and Skills) (Ofsted) (2023) Inspecting Teaching of the Protected Characteristics in Schools. [online] Available at: www.gov.uk/government/publications/inspecting-teaching-of-the-protected-characteristics-in-schools/inspecting-teaching-of-the-protected-characteristics-in-schools (accessed 28 March 2024).

Although this guidance does not focus on trainees, it provides comprehensive guidance from Ofsted on how the teaching of protected characteristics will be inspected in schools.

CHAPTER 5
SUBJECT- AND PHASE-SPECIFIC MENTORING

CHAPTER OBJECTIVES

By the end of this chapter you will understand:

+ how to provide effective subject-specific feedback to trainees;
+ key considerations which are pertinent to specific age phases.

INTRODUCTION

This chapter addresses key aspects of subject- and phase-specific mentoring. It covers the aspects of effective subject-specific feedback and outlines some important age-phase considerations. The chapter also outlines some important approaches that mentors can use to support the development of trainees' knowledge.

PROVIDING FEEDBACK ON SUBSTANTIVE KNOWLEDGE

Substantive knowledge relates to knowledge of the subject concepts, principles and facts. It is the knowledge which makes one subject distinct from another. Examples are listed below:

- In geography, substantive knowledge is the knowledge of places, locations, human and physical geography, and geographical skills and fieldwork.
- Substantive knowledge in science relates to knowledge of chemistry, physics and biology.
- In mathematics, substantive knowledge relates to knowledge of mathematical facts and procedures.
- In history, substantive knowledge is the knowledge of historical concepts such as 'revolution', historical facts and chronology.

Accurate subject knowledge is an essential component of effective teaching. If trainees' subject knowledge is not accurate, pupils will develop inaccurate schemas and subject-specific misconceptions. The ITT curriculum should provide trainees with a thorough 'grounding' in subject knowledge. However, on a one-year ITT programme it is not possible for ITT providers to cover everything that trainees need to know. Subject knowledge is developed through both centre-based training led by the provider and training in school, which is delivered by expert mentors. Trainees are expected to research the subject content thoroughly for the lessons that they are teaching. This should not be a difficult task, given the extensive range of digital resources that are now available. In addition, trainees should be encouraged to join subject associations to keep up to date with their subject knowledge. They can talk to subject leaders in school if they need further support and there will be subject-specific resources also available in school that will support trainees' subject knowledge.

CRITICAL QUESTIONS

- Why is substantive knowledge important?
- Identify a subject that is not listed above. What is the substantive knowledge in that subject?

PROVIDING FEEDBACK ON DISCIPLINARY KNOWLEDGE

Disciplinary knowledge relates to knowledge of how subject experts work within a discipline. The following examples help to illustrate this.

+ Scientists develop scientific questions. They design fair scientific investigations to answer a question. They make predictions, carry out experiments, record results and formulate conclusions.
+ Historians critically evaluate historical evidence. They construct historical claims and arguments.
+ In English, authors evaluate the quality of their writing to consider the impact of their writing on the reader. They re-read and edit their writing to refine it. Readers think critically about the text they are reading.

Trainees' lesson plans often focus on the substantive knowledge that they are teaching, but there is often an insufficient focus on how they will develop pupils' disciplinary knowledge of the subject. Disciplinary knowledge does not need to be evident in every lesson, but it should be integrated into a sequence of lessons. Guided lesson planning with an emphasis on disciplinary knowledge is a useful mentoring strategy to support the development of trainees' disciplinary knowledge. If the disciplinary knowledge is not 'fleshed out' on the lesson plan, it is likely that it will not be sufficiently addressed within a lesson. Mentors might also review trainees' planning across a sequence of lessons to support trainees to reflect on the balance of substantive and disciplinary knowledge across a unit of work.

DEVELOPING SUBJECT KNOWLEDGE IN SCHOOL PLACEMENTS

Some trainees may require additional support with aspects of subject knowledge. Trainees with dyslexia, for example, may need additional coaching to develop their knowledge of phonics and writing. Trainees who have a diagnosis of dyscalculia may require additional coaching in mathematics to support them with their understanding of mathematical facts and processes. Trainees' subject knowledge development takes place through both centre-based training and school-based training. Subject leaders and mentors in school can play an important role in developing trainees' subject knowledge, and opportunities for trainees to meet with leaders should be integrated into placement experiences.

Mentors can also support the development of subject knowledge using the following approaches.

- **Subject-specific tutorials.** These can focus on an aspect of subject knowledge that the trainee is required to teach. They can be delivered by subject leaders.
- **Guided lesson visits.** Expert mentors can visit lessons with trainees. Following a lesson visit, expert mentors can deconstruct the lesson with trainees by isolating the aspects of the lesson where subject knowledge was being taught. Mentors can guide trainees to consider how subject knowledge was being taught and how pupils' subject-specific misconceptions were being addressed in lessons.
- **Guided planning.** Mentors can scaffold trainees' subject knowledge development by co-planning a lesson with the trainees. This might be a useful strategy during the early stages of a placement. Trainees can gradually be expected to plan more independently as the placement progresses.
- **Guided teaching.** Mentors can co-teach a lesson with the trainee and aspects of the subject knowledge in the lesson can be shared between the mentor and the trainee.
- **Providing subject-specific feedback.** Mentors can focus their feedback on trainees' teaching on subject knowledge rather than pedagogical knowledge. Pedagogical knowledge may include the teaching strategies used in the lesson, trainees' use of assessment and trainees' skills in managing pupils' behaviour. There may be times when mentors need to explicitly focus on aspects of pedagogical knowledge. However, using feedback to develop trainees' subject knowledge is a useful mentoring strategy.
- **Setting subject-specific targets.** Mentors should routinely set trainees subject-specific targets. These targets should focus on *content knowledge*, *pedagogical knowledge* and *pedagogical content knowledge*. Content knowledge relates to knowledge of the subject. This is substantive knowledge. Pedagogical knowledge relates to knowledge of effective teaching methods (for example, explicit, direct instruction or enquiry-based approaches). Pedagogical content knowledge relates to knowledge of how to teach a specific subject or topic.
- **Using recorded lessons.** Mentors can use instructional coaching to review recorded lessons. They can use deconstruction to isolate specific aspects of the lesson that they wish the trainee to focus on. Mentors can also video record trainees' lessons. Following the lesson, they can review the recorded lesson with the trainee and isolate specific aspects of content knowledge, pedagogical knowledge or pedagogical content knowledge.

AGE-PHASE CONSIDERATIONS

The following sections outline some age-phase considerations for mentors. These suggestions do not negate the need for mentors to shape the curriculum they provide to trainees to the context of the school.

EARLY YEARS FOUNDATION STAGE

Trainees who are training to teach in the birth to five years phase need to understand how the statutory requirements for this phase are being implemented within the setting. The ITT/ITE curriculum in schools might address the following aspects:

+ Curriculum **planning** for children in the Early Years Foundation Stage: Trainees need to understand how the curriculum in the early years promotes readiness for the subject curriculum in the primary phase. Trainees also need to understand the interconnected nature of learning in the early years, such as understanding how a single activity may be designed to develop children's knowledge across a range of areas of learning.

+ How practitioners ensure a **balance** of adult-led teaching and child-initiated learning: Trainees should understand that both approaches are necessary, but that the balance may shift to more adult-led or adult-guided learning as children progress through the Early Years Foundation Stage.

+ **Adult intervention** in child-initiated learning: Trainees should understand how adults can seize opportunities in children's play to advance children's vocabularies and other aspects of development.

+ Approaches to **assessment** in the early years: Trainees should understand that assessment in the early years is fundamentally different to assessment in the primary phase. Trainees should understand the range of types of evidence that practitioners collect and approaches taken by school leaders to minimise workload for practitioners. Trainees should have opportunities, if possible, to participate in assessment moderation meetings.

+ How to create **enabling environments** which allow children to thrive: This includes the important role of practitioners in creating positive, nurturing environments and the physical environment of an early years classroom. Trainees should also understand how to create effective outdoor environments.

+ How practitioners promote **vocabulary development**: Vocabulary is essential for reading and writing development and it also underpins the whole curriculum. Trainees must understand how practitioners promote vocabulary development through modelling ambitious vocabulary.

+ **Rules and routines**: Trainees need to learn about the importance of establishing rules and routines in the early years. This includes developing an understanding of how skilled adults support children to resolve conflicts and the structure of the day.

+ The role of **sustained shared thinking**: Skilled early years practitioners can seize learning opportunities from conversations *which are initiated by children* to advance their knowledge. This is often referred to as 'sustained shared thinking'. Trainees need to recognise when practitioners are engaging children in periods of sustained shared thinking and learn to practise this technique for themselves.

+ **Early reading**: Trainees should understand how nursery settings lay the foundations for the teaching of synthetic phonics through activities which develop sound awareness, sound discrimination and phonological awareness. Trainees need to learn about the importance of rhyme in developing phonological awareness and ways in which this is promoted, for example through songs and stories.

CRITICAL QUESTIONS

+ A trainee does not value the role of play in learning. They have expressed this several times. They do not plan for child-initiated learning opportunities and focus on planning for adult-led sessions which they are leading. How might you address this?

+ What other learning opportunities do you think are important for trainees in the early years?

CASE STUDY

EARLY VOCABULARY

A mentor observed a guided play activity in a nursery class. The practitioner started to play with the children. The children were playing with a collection of objects in the water. The practitioner used vocabulary such as 'floating' and 'sinking'. The practitioner said: *'Why do you think the feather is floating?'* One child said: *'It is because it is light'*. The practitioner then said: *'Good. It is also flat and that helps it to float. Can heavy objects float?'*. The child *'No, only light things can float'*. The practitioner then showed the child a photograph of a ship which was floating on water. The practitioner said: *'The ship is heavy'*. The child then said: *'I wonder why it can float. I don't know'*. The practitioner then played with the children in the water. She gave them a ball of modelling dough and she asked them to predict what would happen to it when it was placed in the water. The ball sank. She then modelled how to change the shape of the ball into the shape of a ship. She then asked the children to predict what would happen to it when it was placed in the water. The children were amazed to see that it floated.

After the lesson, the mentor asked the trainee to reflect on what they had both observed and to identify the key aspects of pedagogy which had developed the children's knowledge. The mentor isolated each of the aspects of pedagogy, including the practitioner modelling vocabulary, asking questions and using sustained shared thinking. The mentor then introduced the trainee to seminal research on adult intervention in children's play. The mentor had selected the Department for Education research briefing paper by Taggart et al (2015). The mentor then asked the trainee to consider the implications for the trainee's own curriculum planning.

PRIMARY PHASE

Trainees who are training to teach in the primary phase need to learn the following through the ITT/ITE curriculum in schools:

+ All trainees need to learn about the age phases before and after the one in which they are training to teach. Trainees in the primary phase should therefore spend some time in nursery and Reception classes and they should meet with the early years leader to develop their knowledge of this phase. Opportunities for trainees to learn about the curriculum at Key Stage 3 can be facilitated through arranging visits to the local secondary school or through involving trainees in primary–secondary transition activities.

+ Trainees must have opportunities to teach across the **full primary curriculum**. Mentors will need to plan for trainees to teach PE, music and languages, if these are taught by external staff which the school 'buys in' to support curriculum delivery.

+ Trainees should learn about arrangements for **statutory assessment** at Key Stages 1 and 2. They should learn about the statutory assessments (including the phonics screening check) and mark schemes and have opportunities to use mark schemes.

+ Trainees must learn about the school's approach to **monitoring pupils' progress** across the primary curriculum. It is important that trainees learn about the school's approach to assessment in all subjects, including how gaps in learning are identified and addressed. Trainees should be given opportunities to learn how to assess pupils' writing and participate in writing moderation exercises.

+ The multiplication tables check is statutory for all Year 4 pupils registered at state-funded maintained schools, special schools or academies, including free schools, in England. Trainees should learn about how the school implements this and how gaps in knowledge are identified and addressed.

+ Trainees should meet with subject leaders to learn about the process of curriculum design. Trainees should review curriculum plans with subject leaders to understand how the curriculum is designed to ensure that pupils know more, remember more and can do more. They should learn about how subject content is revisited and how curriculum plans are aligned with national curriculum goals.

SYSTEMATIC SYNTHETIC PHONICS AND EARLY READING

On 3–7 or 5–11 ITT programmes, it is important that trainees can observe experts teaching early reading. Trainees must have opportunities to observe synthetic phonics being taught, to plan lessons and lesson sequences and to teach synthetic phonics. Trainees must also receive feedback from expert mentors on their teaching of early reading.

The curriculum in the centre should have introduced trainees to the principles of synthetic phonics, the simple and complex alphabetic code, and the application of synthetic phonics in reading and writing. Trainees should know the research evidence which underpins synthetic phonics, and they should know that synthetic phonics is a time-limited strategy to support the development of word recognition. Trainees should know that although the emphasis is on the development of word recognition in the early stages of reading development, the emphasis shifts to comprehension once children are proficient in word recognition. They should understand the importance of vocabulary development in reading development, and they should know how to teach vocabulary across the curriculum.

The ITE/ITT curriculum in schools should build on the knowledge that trainees have gained in the centre. The school-based curriculum might cover the following aspects:

+ Introducing trainees to the **synthetic phonics scheme**: Trainees need to understand how the scheme works and develop familiarity with the scheme's resources.

+ Introducing the **reading scheme**: Trainees need to understand how the reading scheme aligns with the synthetic phonics scheme to ensure that children are not asked to read words which are outside of their existing phonics knowledge.

+ Learning about **assessment** in early reading: Expert mentors can introduce trainees to the school's approach to assessment in synthetic phonics. Trainees must understand how gaps in learning are identified and the interventions which are provided to close these gaps.

+ Learning about **statutory assessment**: Trainees should learn about the phonics screening check and the assessment of reading in statutory assessment tests. Trainees should have opportunities to review test papers and published mark schemes.

+ Learning about how the school creates a **culture of reading**: Reading is probably *the* most important aspect of the primary curriculum. Reading is the 'gateway' to the rest of the curriculum. It is important that trainees learn how to create a culture of reading. Reading should underpin all subjects in the curriculum, and primary schools should promote enjoyment in reading. Trainees need to learn about how the school is promoting a culture of reading with pupils, staff and parents and about how the school is working in partnership with the community, authors, poets and other organisations to promote reading.

+ **Reading in Key Stage 2**: Trainees need to learn about how reading is taught in Key Stage 2. They need to learn about the interventions that are being implemented to support those children who fall in the lowest 20 per cent of readers.

+ **Reading leaders**: Trainees need to learn about any volunteering opportunities that the school has created to enable pupils to lead on reading, for example through establishing roles such as pupil librarians.

+ **Application of phonics and reading**: Trainees need to learn about how phonics and reading are applied across the curriculum.

CRITICAL QUESTIONS

+ A trainee is nearing the end of their training, and they are in a Key Stage 2 class. They have not yet taught phonics. How might you facilitate this?

+ A trainee is nearing the end of their training and they have not yet taught the full primary curriculum. How might you address this?

SECONDARY PHASE

Trainees who are training to teach in the secondary phase need to learn the following through the ITT/ITE curriculum in schools:

+ Trainees should have opportunities to teach their specialist subject. They should receive mentoring from subject experts to ensure that trainees receive high-quality subject-specific mentoring.

+ Trainees should have opportunities to learn about approaches to curriculum planning and assessment in their specialist subject.

+ Trainees should have opportunities to teach across the full age range in which they are training to teach: This may include teaching, under supervision, some classes who are preparing for public examinations.

- Trainees should have opportunities to undertake observations in the sixth form if the school has one: They should also meet with the sixth-form leader to discuss the sixth-form provision.
- Trainees need to learn about the school's approach to careers education: They need to understand how employability skills are embedded into the subject curriculum and through work experience placements. Trainees need to learn how the school is addressing the Gatsby benchmarks.
- Trainees should have opportunities to observe the teaching of relationships and sex education and health education: In the secondary curriculum, pertinent issues relating to intimate relationships, pornography, consent and substance abuse are addressed. It is important that trainees understand how to teach these potentially sensitive aspects of the curriculum.
- Trainees should have opportunities to observe the use of tutor time.

CRITICAL QUESTIONS

- You are mentoring a secondary trainee. They need some experience teaching in Key Stage 4, but school leaders are reluctant to place them in a Key Stage 4 class because those pupils are studying for GCSEs. How might you address this?
- You are mentoring a trainee who only wants to teach their subject. They do not want to spend time learning about other aspects of the curriculum, such as careers education. How might you address this with the trainee?

CASE STUDY

SYNTHETIC PHONICS

A secondary school had identified a group of pupils in Year 7 who needed intervention in word recognition. These pupils were not reading, and leaders had identified that this was a barrier to their progress across the whole secondary curriculum. The pupils had daily phonics lessons, which also included the application of phonics to reading and writing. The mentor arranged for the trainees to observe these sessions. Working with the reading leader, the trainee then planned a sequence of lessons to support word recognition skills. The reading leader observed the trainee and provided them with feedback on their teaching. The reading leader then carried out some lesson visits with the trainee to help them to learn about the important role that reading plays in all subjects. This helped the trainee to appreciate the value of reading intervention in Year 7.

ALL PHASES

Regardless of phase, trainees should, within the content of the ITT/ITE curriculum in schools, learn about the following:

+ The school's approach to **safeguarding** children and young people: It is particularly important that trainees know how to recognise possible abuse, how to report concerns and what to say to children or young people if a disclosure is made.

+ The leadership of **Special Educational Needs and/or Disabilities**: Trainees need to know how leaders and teachers identify Special Educational Needs and/or Disabilities (SEND), what provision is available for pupils with SEND and how leaders ensure that pupils with SEND are provided with an ambitious curriculum. They need to know to adapt their teaching to support pupils in their classes who have SEND.

+ The school's approach to managing **behaviour**: All trainees need to know how to address low-level disruption and which strategies to use for managing more challenging behaviour. Trainees need to know how the school manages exclusions or suspensions and how to implement the school policy for behaviour during lessons.

+ Addressing pupil **absence**: Pupil absence has become an increasing concern post Covid-19. Too many children are not in schools, and some are on part-time timetables (Ofsted, 2023). Trainees need to know about what the school is doing to address pupil absence and how to respond when pupils arrive late to lessons.

+ Understanding the use of **pupil premium**: Trainees should understand how pupil premium funding is used and how the impact of this funding is measured.

> **RESEARCH**
>
> According to Coe et al (2014), there is a strong relationship between teacher subject knowledge and student outcomes:
>
> *The most effective teachers have deep knowledge of the subjects they teach, and when teachers' knowledge falls below a certain level it is a significant impediment to students' learning. As well as a strong understanding of the material being taught, teachers must also understand the ways students think about the content, be able to evaluate the thinking behind students' own methods and identify students' common misconceptions.*
>
> (Coe et al, 2014, p 2)

SUMMARY

This chapter has outlined the important role of the mentor in providing trainees with subject-specific feedback and subject-specific targets. The chapter has also outlined important age-phase considerations.

> **CHECKLIST**
>
> + Subject-specific feedback and subject-specific targets support the development of trainees' subject knowledge.
>
> + Although the Teachers' Standards apply to all age phases, there are important age-phase considerations for mentors and trainees.
>
> + There are also important considerations for all trainees irrespective of the phase in which they are training to teach.

FURTHER READING

Blog

Teach First (2022) *We Need Effective Teacher Mentoring — Here's 6 Ways It Can Make a Lasting Difference.* [online] Available at: www.teachfirst.org.uk/blog/6-ways-effective-teacher-mentoring (accessed 28 March 2024).

This is a useful blog which outlines the components of effective mentoring.

Ofsted research review series

Office for Standards in Education, Children's Services and Skills (Ofsted) (2021) Curriculum Research Reviews: A Series of Reviews by Ofsted Looking at the Research Evidence Currently Available about Different Curriculum Subjects. [online] Available at: www.gov.uk/government/collections/curriculum-research-reviews (accessed 28 March 2024).

The Ofsted curriculum reviews are essential reading for trainees and mentors. They outline the subject knowledge in each subject.

CHAPTER 6
SUBJECT-SPECIFIC FEEDBACK: A TOOLKIT FOR MENTORS

> ## CHAPTER OBJECTIVES
>
> **By the end of this chapter you will understand:**
>
> + what is meant by subject-specific feedback;
> + the characteristics of effective subject-specific feedback in different subjects.

INTRODUCTION

When you are carrying out lesson visits and undertaking lesson observations of trainees there is often so much that you might comment on in your feedback. Often, particularly in primary ITE, mentors will comment on aspects of *generic pedagogy*, including teaching methods, use of assessment and behaviour management, with very little emphasis on the trainees' subject knowledge. Although pedagogy is important, *pedagogical content knowledge* is also a critical factor in determining teacher effectiveness (Coe et al, 2014) and therefore it warrants greater attention in mentor feedback. This chapter provides a toolkit of resources to support mentors in developing greater subject specificity in their feedback.

The checklists provided should not be used as tick lists by mentors during lesson visits and observations. Instead, they should be used to support discussions with trainees about their subject knowledge.

THE IMPORTANCE OF SUBJECT KNOWLEDGE

According to Coe et al:

The most effective teachers have deep knowledge of the subjects they teach, and when teachers' knowledge falls below a certain level it is a significant impediment to students' learning. As well as a strong understanding of the material being taught, teachers must also understand the ways students think about the content, be able to evaluate the thinking behind students' own methods, and identify students' common misconceptions.

(Coe et al, 2014, p 2)

An Education Endowment Foundation (2021a) report highlights the use of feedback as an important component of effective teacher development. However, given the importance of subject knowledge in teacher effectiveness, feedback which lacks subject specificity is missing a crucial component which can support trainee teachers to become better teachers.

+ **Content knowledge** relates to knowledge of the subject facts, principles, laws and concepts.
+ **Pedagogical knowledge** relates to knowledge of teaching and assessment strategies, as well as generic knowledge about behaviour management and adaptive teaching.
+ **Pedagogical content knowledge** relates to knowledge of how to teach a specific subject.

It is likely that mentor feedback will address all three aspects across the duration of a school placement, but it is not necessary to focus on all types of knowledge in a single lesson.

CONTENT KNOWLEDGE

Content knowledge refers to both substantive and disciplinary knowledge. The following two sections address each of these in turn.

SUBSTANTIVE KNOWLEDGE

If trainees do not have good enough knowledge of the subject content (substantive knowledge), it is likely that their explanations to pupils will be unclear, they will teach incorrect information and this will result in pupils developing subject-specific misconceptions. In addition, if subject knowledge is weak, trainees will be unlikely to be able to answer pupils' questions. Mentors should always address inaccuracies in subject knowledge, and it is reasonable to address these immediately in the lesson (in a sensitive way) so that the quality of pupils' education is not affected.

DISCIPLINARY KNOWLEDGE

Sometimes you might find that trainees need more support in developing their disciplinary knowledge within subjects. For example, it is not uncommon for less experienced teachers to set up enquiry tasks in the classroom without first adequately ensuring that pupils have learned the prerequisite knowledge and skills to undertake the enquiry. In science, the scientific process is the approach used by scientists. Scientists make predictions, plan fair tests, carry out investigations, collect results, analyse data, formulate conclusions and communicate their findings. Each of these components of disciplinary knowledge needs to be taught explicitly and directly before pupils can be asked to design and carry out a full scientific investigation. These components of knowledge need to be sequenced across the science curriculum and each component needs to be practised until pupils are secure with the knowledge or skill. Trainees with weaker disciplinary knowledge might not recognise the importance of explicitly teaching and scaffolding pupils' disciplinary knowledge before they are asked to work more independently on enquiry tasks. Trainees with weaker disciplinary knowledge might not give adequate attention to it during lesson planning, instead focusing exclusively on developing pupils' substantive knowledge.

CRITICAL QUESTIONS

+ When might you focus more on trainees' subject knowledge?
+ When might you focus less on trainee subject knowledge?
+ Lesson feedback is one mentoring approach for developing trainees' subject knowledge. What other approaches might mentors use to develop trainees' subject knowledge?

PEDAGOGICAL KNOWLEDGE

Pedagogical knowledge includes knowledge of specific teaching and assessment strategies, including modelling, explanations, questioning, pupil activities and use of quizzes in lessons. Mentors need to check trainees' planning and teaching to ensure that the choice of teaching strategies and activities for pupils enables the pupils to learn the intended curriculum.

CRITICAL QUESTIONS

+ When might mentors focus more on pedagogical knowledge than subject knowledge?
+ This section has provided some examples of pedagogical knowledge that teachers need. What other examples can you think of?

PEDAGOGICAL CONTENT KNOWLEDGE

Pedagogical content knowledge relates to knowledge of how to teach a subject. Specific pedagogical approaches are used in some subjects. For example, geographical fieldwork is associated with geography. In English, shared composition is a powerful way to teach writing. Concrete or pictorial representations can be powerful in mathematics, particularly when learning about abstract mathematical concepts such as place value. Concept cartoons can be a powerful way of teaching pupils about scientific concepts and processes.

CRITICAL QUESTIONS

+ What pedagogical content knowledge might trainees require in other subjects?
+ What is the difference between pedagogical content knowledge and pedagogical knowledge?

TOOLKITS FOR MENTORS

The following tables provide mentors with a summary of the subject knowledge that trainees might be demonstrating when teaching specific subjects. Trainees are not required to demonstrate all the features listed in each table. The information in the tables has been taken from the Ofsted curriculum research reviews: www.gov.uk/government/collections/curriculum-research-reviews

Table 6.1 Subject-specific feedback: synthetic phonics

Evidence in lessons	
Use of correct vocabulary – phoneme, grapheme, digraph, split digraph, adjacent consonants	Revisiting previous phonemes
Correct enunciation of phonemes	Challenge – decoding multi-syllabic words
Modelling of blending of reading	Counting the phonemes in words
Modelling of segmenting for spelling, including the use of phoneme frames for segmenting	Using flash cards
Independent opportunities for pupils to blend or segment	'Robot' talk
Opportunities to apply phonics knowledge through reading and writing a caption or sentence	Evidence of oral blending and oral segmenting
Scheme fidelity – implementing the scheme in the way it is intended	Unfamiliar vocabulary is explained to pupils
Addressing misconceptions	Accurate teaching of common exception words
Clear lesson structure (for example, revisit, teach, practice and apply)	Use of actions to accompany phonemes (scheme dependent)
Inclusion of nonsense words if relevant	The new phoneme appears in different positions in words and teachers draw pupils' attention to the phoneme position

Table 6.2 Subject-specific feedback: English

	Evidence in lessons
Explicit teaching of spoken language	Pupils have opportunities to read together as a class: maximum participation
Modelling of standard English	Modelling metacognitive thinking: teacher models thinking out loud to compose sentences and models editing writing to improve it
Supports pupils to apply their phonics knowledge in reading and writing tasks	Effective questioning to encourage pupils to critically evaluate texts, including characters
Provides pupils with background knowledge to support comprehension activities; range of reading comprehension strategies are explicitly taught	Powerful literature is carefully chosen for a purpose – for example, poetry, novels, playscripts
Choice of text is well-considered: texts are ambitious and chosen on literary merit	Oral composition is modelled and encouraged
There is a curriculum for reading for pleasure	Pupils have enough time to practise spoken language, reading and writing tasks
Explicit teaching of transcription skills	Self- and peer assessment of writing are encouraged
Explicit teaching of composition skills – modelling of writing through teacher modelling and shared composition	Pupils are encouraged to consider the impact of their writing on the reader as they write
Grammar is taught explicitly and in context	Pupils are encouraged to read texts and to consider the writer's intentions for the reader as they read
Explicit teaching of spelling; spelling is taught in context	Scaffolding is evident in the lesson – for example, '*I do, we do, you do*'

Table 6.3 Subject-specific feedback: mathematics

Evidence in lessons	
Accurate teaching of *declarative knowledge* – mathematical facts, principles and concepts	Checking on previous mathematical knowledge
Accurate teaching of *procedural knowledge* – for example, teaching the correct steps to answer a mathematical problem	Scaffolding and fading – for example, '*I do, we do, you do*'
Accurate teaching of *conditional knowledge* – for example, teaching mathematical reasoning and problem solving	Includes concrete and pictorial representations to explain abstract mathematical content
Explicit teaching of mathematical vocabulary	Testing to build mathematical fluency
Mathematical misconceptions are addressed	Highlights mathematical patterns
Expert *modelling* of mathematics knowledge	Encourages pupils to demonstrate metacognitive strategies – for example, showing their working out, self-checking their answers
Planned use of assessment in the lesson to check pupils' mathematical understanding, for example using a hinge question	Reduces cognitive load to reduce the load on the working memory
Teaching children to systematically apply/use mathematical strategies rather than rely on guesswork	Encourages mathematical resilience – for example, by encouraging perseverance when pupils become 'stuck'
Providing pupils with worked examples of mathematics	Requiring pupils to explain their answers – for example, 'prove it'
Providing opportunities for purposeful practice and overlearning to develop procedural fluency	Expects all pupils to learn the mathematical content

Table 6.4 Subject-specific feedback: science

Evidence in lessons	
Accurate substantive knowledge	Trainees use effective questioning to promote scientific thinking
Explicit teaching of disciplinary knowledge before pupils are asked to work scientifically, for example teaching pupils background knowledge of animals before asking them to carry out a sorting or grouping task	Health and safety are reinforced
Working scientifically is a key pedagogical approach	Clear behavioural expectations are established during the execution of practical work
Use of correct vocabulary, for example *substance, apparatus*	Pupils have opportunities to identify different ways of exploring a scientific question and to follow these ideas through in practical work
Demonstrations are used as a key teaching strategy	Trainee explanations are accurate
Scientific misconceptions are addressed, and the trainee does not develop misconceptions in pupils	Trainees use 'real-world' examples to exemplify abstract scientific concepts, facts and principles
Practical work has a clear focus on an aspect of substantive knowledge, for example a scientific concept, fact, relationships, or a model/theory	Pupils learn about significant discoveries in science and significant scientists where relevant
Pupils record science through drawing, writing and other forms	Effective use of assessment to check pupils' scientific knowledge – for example, using questioning during practical work
Pupils have opportunities to share their scientific ideas and reasoning	Pupils record science in lists, tables, diagrams and graphs
The science subject content is applied to the real world where possible	Disciplinary knowledge is planned for and accurate

CASE STUDY

ELECTRICITY

Charlie is teaching a Key Stage 2 class about electricity. In previous lessons the children have been introduced to different items which use mains electricity and items which run from batteries. They can name the components in an electric circuit and they know that a complete circuit is needed to make a bulb light. In this lesson, Charlie wants the children to learn about the effects of varying the number of components in a circuit. He demonstrates how to create an electric circuit with specific scientific equipment. He then asks the children to construct their own circuits to make a bulb light. The pupils do this and show delight in making a bulb light. Charlie then asks them to identify different ways of breaking the circuit to turn the bulb off and on. The children suggest ideas and he records these on the whiteboard. He then asks them to try one of these ideas. Next, Charlie asks them to predict what will happen to the brightness of the bulb if they put an extra wire and use two bulbs in the circuit instead of one. Some pupils predict that the bulbs will glow brighter, some think that there will be no change and some think that the bulbs will go dim. Charlie asks them to test this out. The pupils do this and notice that the bulbs are dim. He then explains to the pupils that this is because the bulbs are sharing the power from the battery. Charlie praises the children for their responses.

CRITICAL QUESTIONS

+ What feedback would you give to Charlie?
+ What target would you give him?
+ What scientific misconceptions did the children demonstrate?
+ What does Charlie need to do in the next lesson?

Table 6.5 Subject-specific feedback: history

Evidence in lessons	
Accurate substantive knowledge of history	Teacher explanations of historical knowledge are accurate and clear
Disciplinary knowledge is explicitly taught	Effective questioning supports pupils to developer deeper historical knowledge
Pupils undertake enquiry after they have the prerequisite substantive and disciplinary knowledge to enable them to do this successfully	Specific historical misconceptions are addressed
'Fingertip' knowledge is taught – for example, key knowledge the pupils need to remember	Gaps in historical knowledge are identified and addressed
Substantive historical concepts are explained clearly – for example, trade, empire, monarchy	Pupils develop in-depth rather than superficial knowledge – for example, learning about the pyramids does not provide a depth of knowledge about Ancient Egypt
Chronological knowledge is a focus so that pupils know when events happened and what came before and after – for example, order of periods, dates and events	Pupils learn about the wider historical context when learning about significant people from the past – for example, they learn about the African American civil rights context when studying Rosa Parks
Pupils know what core knowledge they need to remember	Pupils communicate their historical knowledge in a range of ways – including, but not limited to, writing
Historical misconceptions are addressed	Stories are used to bring the past to life
Enquiry starts with a question	Formative assessment identifies whether pupils have learned the intended curriculum
Pupils use primary and secondary sources	Lessons have a clear historical focus

Table 6.6 Subject-specific feedback: geography

Evidence in lessons	
Accurate substantive knowledge – location, place, human and physical features and geographical skills	Pupils know the geographical knowledge they must remember
Procedural knowledge is developed through fieldwork	Geographical enquiry starts with a question
Pupils develop map skills through exploring a range of maps, globes and atlases, and they are shown how to construct maps and decode information from them	Effective assessment in geography identifies misconceptions or gaps in learning
Range of rich resources – for example, aerial photographs, digital maps, satellite images	Learning is connected to previous topics
Teacher uses clear and accurate geographical explanations	All pupils learn the same content – high ambition for all
Teacher uses effective questioning to deepen pupils' geographical knowledge	Geographical knowledge is explicitly taught and developed before pupils are asked to apply it
Teacher encourages pupils to 'think like a geographer'	Links to other subjects are made – for example, the natural sciences
Explicit teaching of substantive concepts – for example, town, suburb, climate	Pupils develop a depth of knowledge rather than superficial knowledge
Pupils learn about places through 'different lenses' rather than developing a single perspective of a place	Pupils learn about a specific region rather than a country to develop a depth of knowledge
Geographical misconceptions are addressed	Pupils begin to understand the relationships between locational knowledge, place knowledge and human and physical features – for example, the location of a place affects the climate

Table 6.7 Subject-specific feedback: art and design

Evidence in lessons	
Explicit modelling of art techniques, for example, in drawing, painting and sculpture	Pupils can work on a piece of art over time
Pupils develop *technical proficiency* (practical knowledge)	Pupils have opportunities to compare art
Pupils develop *theoretical knowledge* – for example, learning about artists in context	Pupils self-assess their work
Pupils develop *disciplinary knowledge* – for example, learning how art is discussed and evaluated	Peer assessment is sometimes used
Subject-specific vocabulary is explicitly taught – for example, cross-hatching, stippling	Effective questioning deepens pupils' knowledge of art – for example, asking pupils about the shape of the face, nose, eyes and position of these features during the modelling of a self-portrait
Pupils learn about the contexts which influence the work of artists – for example, they study the work of Van Gogh but also learn about the post-impressionism movement	Pupils have adequate time to practise art
Pupils learn about how social, historical, cultural and political contexts influence art and design	Lessons are broken down into small components of knowledge which are well sequenced across a series of lessons
Pupils produce creative outputs	Pupils use sketchbooks to practise techniques
Pupils have opportunities for repeated practice to develop technical proficiency	Pupils take responsibility for organising equipment and clearing away
Instruction is scaffolded – '*I do, we do, you do*'	Pupils take care of equipment and comply with health and safety expectations

Table 6.8 Subject-specific feedback: design and technology

Evidence in lessons	
Pupils have opportunities to evaluate existing products	Technical vocabulary is taught explicitly – for example, bench hook
The lesson is part of a sequence of learning – product analysis, design, make and evaluate	The skill of designing is explicitly modelled and pupils practise designing in a range of ways, for example using mood boards or designing by making prototypes
Pupils design and make products for a specific purpose	Pupils learn about the role of technology in society
Technical skills are explicitly modelled by the teacher	Pupils learn about how technology has changed over time and how it has influenced designing and products
Pupils use evaluation throughout the design and technology process	Subject misconceptions and gaps in learning are addressed through effective use of assessment
Pupils study the work of designers and engineers and learn about the contexts which influenced their work	Lessons are broken down into components of knowledge
Pupils are shown worked examples of products	Adaptations are in place so that all pupils can learn the same curriculum content
Pupils self-assess their designs and products against specific criteria	Pupils have time to engage in practical work
Pupils peer assess their designs and products against specific criteria	Pupils are encouraged to work with care and precision and to persevere when things go wrong
Pupils design and make products after they have gained the knowledge (substantive and disciplinary) to enable them to undertake the task	Health and safety is reinforced from the outset

CASE STUDY

COOKING

In a Key Stage 3 class Jamila is teaching pupils about bread. She is specifically focusing on different types of bread. Jamila introduces different bread types on the whiteboard. Pupils then complete a sensory activity in which they taste different types of bread. They do not record anything, but they discuss in pairs whether they liked different types of bread. The pupils start to demonstrate signs of low-level disruption after a short time. Some of the pupils started to talk about what their plans were for that evening. Some pupils decided that they did not want to complete the sensory activity. Some pupils started to push others as they moved around the different sensory 'stations'. Jamila did not intervene. At the end of the lesson, the mentor gave Jamila some feedback. She focused exclusively on the low-level disruption and she provided Jamila with some useful strategies to help with behaviour management in future lessons.

CRITICAL QUESTIONS

+ What could Jamila have done at the start of the lesson to communicate high expectations?
+ What are the possible effects of not intervening when pupils demonstrate low-level disruption?
+ How might low-level disruption impact on learning?
+ What subject-specific feedback would you have given Jamila?
+ What target would you have given?

Table 6.9 Subject-specific feedback: music

Evidence in lessons	
Tacit knowledge is developed by encouraging pupils to give a response to a piece of music	Effective formative assessment identifies gaps in learning and misconceptions, which are then addressed
Procedural knowledge is developed: knowledge of how to perform a musical task	All pupils learn the same ambitious music curriculum
Declarative knowledge is accurately taught – knowledge of musical eras, styles, performers, composers	Explicit teaching of musical vocabulary
Pupils have the underpinning component knowledge required to undertake a specific musical task	The music curriculum is ambitious and provides pupils with cultural capital – for example, learning about orchestras, musical eras and styles
Expert teacher modelling	Pupils learn about musicians within the social, political and cultural contexts which have influenced their music
Teacher provides pupils with feedback on their musical responses	The music curriculum addresses aspects of equality and inclusion – for example, race and disability
Pupils have adequate time to practise making music	High standards are expected
Depth of learning is encouraged – for example, by limiting the range of instruments that pupils play and focusing on mastery of the ones selected	Pupils take care of musical equipment
Expert guidance is given to pupils	Pupils have opportunities to compose music in groups
The teacher focuses the pupils on improving the quality of their musical responses	Self- and peer assessment is integrated into lessons

Table 6.10 Subject-specific feedback: physical education

Evidence in lessons	
Motor competence is developed through the explicit teaching of fundamental movement skills	Games should be taught after pupils have the underpinning knowledge and skills required to participate in the game
Explicit teaching of rules, strategies and tactics	Competition is introduced at the right time
Pupils learn about the relationship between physical activity, physical health and mental health	Self-assessment is used by pupils to identify what they have done well and what they need to improve
Links are made with human science – for example, muscles, organs	Peer assessment is used
Pupils develop declarative knowledge – '*I know that ...*'	Movements and performances are video recorded, and pupils subsequently evaluate these
Pupils develop procedural knowledge – '*I know how to ...*'	PE is viewed as a broad subject; it is not reduced to sport
Powerful demonstrations are used: teacher modelling	Teacher uses clear, precise explanations
Pupils have opportunities to practise, refine and revisit knowledge and skills	All pupils are included and participate – including those with SEND
Teacher provides pupils with purposeful feedback during the lesson	Warm-ups and cool downs are systematically integrated into lessons
50–80 per cent of lesson time should be devoted to pupils moving	Pupils have opportunities to take short rests

Table 6.11 Subject-specific feedback: religious education

Evidence in lessons	
Substantive knowledge is accurate – knowledge of religions or non-religious traditions	Effective questioning deepens pupils' knowledge about religious and non-religious traditions
Subject concepts are explicitly taught – for example, prayer, sacred, ritual, incarnation, sacrifice	Links are made between subject content and pupils' everyday lives
Subject-specific vocabulary is explicitly taught	Pupils communicate their knowledge in a range of formats, including writing
Teaching focuses on developing pupils' knowledge *about* religion; it does not induct them into a religious tradition	Explanations are clear
Pupils have the opportunity to reflect to build up their personal knowledge	Pupils are encouraged to ask questions
Pupils learn about ways of knowing RE – for example, through enquiry (using artefacts, stories, photographs, site visits etc)	Enquiry in RE begins with a question
Pupils retrieve prior knowledge	Pupils have the substantive knowledge needed to undertake enquiry
Pupils study content in depth	Links are made between different beliefs and traditions to identify similarities and differences
Teacher makes links/comparisons between different topics	Pupils learn about a range of religious and non-religious traditions
Assessment is used to identify gaps in learning	Stereotypes are explicitly challenged

Table 6.12 Subject-specific feedback: personal, social and health education

Evidence in lessons	
Use of distancing techniques – for example, using puppets, stories or case studies to talk about issues	Assessment is used well to identify gaps in learning or misconceptions
Pupils' responses are sensitively addressed	Where relevant, the legislative context is included in lessons – for example, the Equality Act 2010
Different opinions are valued and respected	Links are made with local, regional and national organisations and services where appropriate
Substantive knowledge is accurate	Specific vocabulary is explicitly taught
Pupils are warned that specific content may be sensitive	Explanations are accurate, clear and concise
Case studies are used to exemplify issues	The lesson supports the development of critical thinking
Videos are used to exemplify issues	Pupils are encouraged to debate issues
Visiting speakers from the community enrich the curriculum	Pupils are encouraged to justify their opinions
Subject association material is used	Prejudice is always challenged
Questioning is used effectively to deepen pupils' knowledge	Pupils are introduced to pertinent subject-specific research

Table 6.13 Subject-specific feedback: languages

Evidence in lessons	
Explicit teaching of vocabulary	Authentic opportunities for pupils to listen to the target language
Explicit teaching of grammar	Opportunities for pupils to write in the target language
Explicit teaching of phonics	Use of authentic written text, for example newspaper articles in the target language
Awareness of cognitive load by limiting exposure to new content	Exposure to the target language which aligns with the stage pupils have reached in the language curriculum
Teacher models correct pronunciation of vocabulary	Addressing errors – for example, by recasting
Teacher gives priority to teaching high-frequency words	Using assessment to identify gaps in learning
Teacher gives priority to teaching topic-related words	Link new learning to previous learning
Opportunities to revisit prior learning	Retrieval of prior learning
Opportunities for pupils to speak in the target language	Enough time to practise working with the target language
Opportunities for pupils to read the target language	Use of target language for classroom routines – for example, entering and leaving the classroom

CRITICAL QUESTIONS

+ What might be the challenges in relation to securing appropriate subject-specific mentoring in secondary schools?
+ Why might subject mentoring in primary schools be particularly challenging to secure and how might this be overcome?

RESEARCH

Research on mentor feedback has found that:

+ feedback is often superficial (Land, 2018);
+ feedback is often not subject specific (Soares and Lock, 2007);
+ mentors do not tend to use feedback to develop trainees' conceptual disciplinary understanding (Healy et al, 2020).

SUMMARY

This chapter has provided a practical toolkit to mentors to support with developing subject-specific feedback and target setting. The features listed in the tables will not be present in every lesson. Mentors are best placed to decide whether they need to focus on content knowledge, pedagogical content knowledge or pedagogical knowledge in mentor feedback and target setting (either one or a combination of these), and it is likely that this will be lesson dependent.

CHECKLIST

+ Substantive knowledge includes knowledge of the facts, principles, laws and concepts which underpin the subject.
+ Pedagogical content knowledge relates to knowledge of how to teach a subject.
+ Pedagogical knowledge relates to knowledge of general teaching and assessment approaches.

FURTHER READING

Ofsted subject reports

Office for Standards in Education, Children's Services and Skills (Ofsted) (2021) Curriculum Research Reviews: A Series of Reviews by Ofsted Looking at the Research Evidence Currently Available about Different Curriculum Subjects. [online] Available at: www.gov.uk/government/collections/curriculum-research-reviews#subject-reports (accessed 28 March 2024).

These reports provide useful subject-specific guidance for teachers. In particular, they outline the different subject knowledge types within each subject.

Useful Ofsted webinar

Office for Standards in Education, Children's Services and Skills (Ofsted) (2022) Initial Teacher Education Curriculum Roadshow. [online] Available at: www.youtube.com/watch?v=zlTkRpQZed8 (accessed 28 March 2024).

CHAPTER 7
ASSESSING TRAINEE PROGRESS AND TARGET SETTING

> **CHAPTER OBJECTIVES**
>
> **By the end of this chapter you will understand:**
> + how to assess trainees' progress;
> + how to design effective targets for trainees.

INTRODUCTION

Mentors in school play a crucial role in assessing trainees' progress. They play a dual role in relation to supporting trainees' development and making judgements about their competency as teachers. This can sometimes be difficult for mentors to navigate, especially in cases where trainees are not making enough progress. Mentors may feel as though they are gatekeepers to the profession. Their role is to support trainees, but at the same time be responsible for upholding professional standards. Although these seemingly conflicting roles can be challenging, it is important to remember that the ITE provider is responsible for recommending Qualified Teacher Status and not the mentor. This should alleviate pressure once mentors recognise that they are not responsible for the final assessment of a trainee against the Teachers' Standards.

This chapter outlines approaches for assessing trainees' progress during school placements. It stresses the need for mentors to consider a range of forms of evidence, and also considers effective target setting.

ASSESSING TRAINEES' PROGRESS THROUGH THE ITE CURRICULUM

Assessment is a process through which mentors can evaluate whether trainees are making adequate progress through the ITE curriculum. It is important that mentors do not apply the Teachers' Standards prematurely when assessing trainees' progress. The Teachers' Standards are summative and should therefore only be applied at the end of the training programme. Interim assessments are intended to be used to identify if trainees are 'on track' against the expectations of the ITE curriculum at a particular stage. The ITE curriculum should identify the expected milestones that trainees are expected to reach. For trainees following a one-year programme, progress against these milestones will typically be evaluated at the end of the first, second and third terms of the training programme. For trainees studying on undergraduate courses, progress is typically evaluated at the end of each year, although it is for providers to determine the number of assessment points that trainees need to pass through.

The Initial Teacher Training and Early Career Framework (ITTECF) sets out the minimum knowledge that trainees must learn. Providers will typically break down the broad statements in this framework into smaller components and assess trainees against those. Some of the content will be assessed by the ITE provider and some content will be assessed in schools by mentors. It is therefore useful if providers create a *data dashboard* for each trainee. The dashboard can show each of the milestones which trainees must pass and indicate whether trainees are 'on track' against each milestone. The value of a data dashboard is that all stakeholders (the provider, the trainee and the mentor) can view the dashboard to identify whether trainees are 'on track' and whether they need further support to achieve a specific milestone. Some of the milestones will be achieved in school and others will be achieved through completing assignments and tests. A dashboard will allow mentors to identify whether a trainee is 'on track' against each of the milestones that they should have achieved prior to going into school. If the trainee requires more support with specific milestones, mentors can then design the school-based ITE curriculum to provide trainees with bespoke support on the milestones they have not yet achieved. An example of a data dashboard is shown in Figure 7.1.

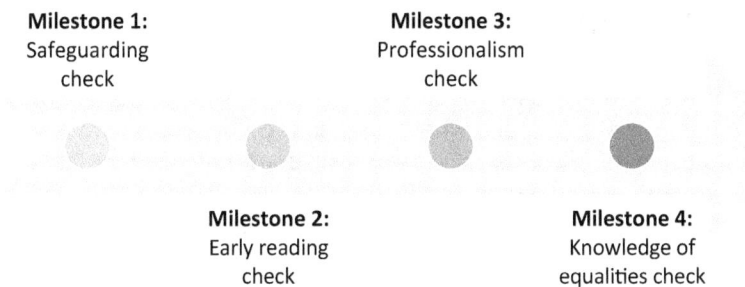

Figure 7.1 Example of a partial assessment tracker

CRITICAL QUESTIONS

+ What essential components of knowledge do you think need to be assessed before a trainee is awarded Qualified Teacher Status?
+ How many assessment points do you think there should be on an ITT programme?
+ Is it necessary to assess everything that a trainee needs to learn in the ITE curriculum?

FOCUSING ON ASSESSMENTS

Mentors typically use a variety of strategies to assess trainees' progress against the ITE curriculum. These may include:

+ lesson visits;
+ professional discussions;
+ reviewing a range of documentary evidence, for example trainees' lesson planning, reflections/evaluations, pupils' work and trainee assessments of pupils' learning;
+ conversations with pupils.

It is important for mentors to make a rounded assessment of trainees' progress. Single lesson visits are not a reliable indicator of teacher quality. It is also important for trainees to recognise that they need to demonstrate that they are consistently meeting the professional competencies, not just when their mentor is observing them.

LESSON VISITS

A lesson visit should be long enough to enable you to identify what the trainee is doing well and what they need to do next to lead to further improvement. However, a lesson visit does not need to last for the full duration of a lesson. The focus of the lesson visit will depend on what you and/or the trainee have identified as a specific aspect to evaluate. This might link to a previous lesson visit in which you identified areas for improvement. Although the trainee's subject knowledge should always generally be a focus of all lesson visits, it is best to limit the foci so that you are not trying to evaluate too many things.

During a lesson visit, you will be able to ascertain very quickly the relationships between the trainee and the pupils. It is important to establish that the trainee can create a calm and safe learning environment and that they make effective use of lesson time. You might choose to focus on the trainee's subject knowledge and specific pedagogical approaches that they utilise within their lesson. Aspects which you may wish to comment on are suggested below.

+ Is the curriculum ambitious for all pupils and adapted to meet the needs of pupils with SEND?
+ Is the curriculum planned and sequenced to enable pupils to develop cumulative knowledge?
+ Does the trainee have strong subject knowledge?
+ Does the trainee present subject matter clearly, promoting appropriate discussion about the subject matter being taught?
+ Does the choice of pedagogical approaches enable pupils to learn the intended curriculum?
+ Does the trainee check pupils' understanding systematically?
+ Does the trainee address misconceptions accurately?
+ Does the trainee provide pupils with feedback?
+ Do pupils have consistently positive attitudes to learning?
+ Do the resources support pupils to learn the intended curriculum?
+ How are reading and vocabulary prioritised in the lesson?

This is not intended as a checklist for mentors to follow during lesson visits. Mentors may choose to focus on a single aspect that they have previously coached the trainee in.

CASE STUDY

LESSON VISITS

Peter was a trainee on a one-year training programme. The mentor had raised concerns about Peter's lesson planning. The planning was scant and did not break down the subject knowledge components in lessons. Peter did not plan assessment tasks into lessons and did not identify, at the planning stage, key questions that he needed to ask the pupils. However, it became evident that when a lesson visit was undertaken, Peter's lesson planning was detailed and included all necessary components. Peter had assumed that he just needed to perform when he was being observed.

The mentor met with pupils with their exercise books. Peter was invited into this session as an observer. The mentor asked the pupils questions about the curriculum that they had been learning over the duration of Peter's professional practice. The pupils could not answer questions which attempted to elicit their subject knowledge. They could not define subject-specific terminology, they did not understand subject concepts and they knew very few facts. However, in the lessons which were prepared well the pupils knew more.

The mentor used the discussion as an opportunity to talk with Peter about having consistently high expectations. Without this, pupils will not make progress. Including the pupils in the evidence was powerful. Peter immediately realised that he needed to work harder. During his subsequent teaching, there was a dramatic improvement and Peter met the professional expectations of the placement.

PROFESSIONAL DISCUSSIONS

Professional discussions can be used to discuss lesson visits. Mentors should aim to use skillful questioning to guide trainees to reflect on their own development rather than just communicating with the trainee their thoughts on the lesson. Examples of effective questions might include the following:

+ Can you explain to me how this lesson fits into a learning sequence?

- How do you know that the pupils know more, remember more and can do more as a result of this lesson?

- I noticed the adaptations for pupils with SEND. How effective do you think these were?

- I saw that Susie was starting to lose focus during the main teaching input. What might you do next time to maintain her engagement?

- You modelled the mathematics and then you asked the pupils to work independently on the strategy that you modelled. You mentioned to me in the lesson that some pupils were not clear on the steps in the calculation. What scaffolding could you have put into the lesson before you sent them off to work on their own? When is the right time to remove scaffolding? Let's review Rosenshine's principles of effective instruction to see where scaffolding fits into that model.

Professional discussions can also take place at other times, for example during weekly mentor meetings or when other experts in school meet trainees to discuss safeguarding, synthetic phonics, behaviour, assessment, the subject curriculum, early years or SEND. Some ITE providers are increasingly providing mentors and other experts with a 'script' to frame these professional discussions. These discussions are sometimes referred to as tutorials.

CRITICAL QUESTIONS

- What are the advantages of mentors using a script to structure their conversations with mentors?

- Are there any disadvantages? Explain your answer.

DOCUMENTARY EVIDENCE

During their time in school, trainees will develop a range of documentary evidence to support their professional practice. This evidence may include samples of lesson planning, reflective evaluations, assessments of pupils' learning, samples of marking and communications with parents. This evidence can be used to form a holistic assessment of the trainee. It is particularly important for mentors to check trainees' lesson planning to ensure that trainees have broken down the subject knowledge into well-sequenced 'chunks' of knowledge for pupils. It is also important that trainees' lesson plans demonstrate that they are planning to develop pupils' disciplinary knowledge as well as their substantive knowledge. The following examples may help mentors in this aspect.

+ In science, does trainees' planning indicate that pupils are working scientifically across sequences of lessons?
+ Is there evidence in their lesson planning that pupils have opportunities to develop their knowledge of historical enquiry?
+ In English, does trainees' planning indicate that pupils have opportunities to think like writers?
+ Does lesson planning in mathematics ensure that pupils can think like mathematicians, for example through investigating, reasoning, problem solving, justifying and proving?

CRITICAL QUESTIONS

+ Some schools provide trainees with ready-made slides for lessons to reduce workload. What are the advantages and disadvantages of this approach?
+ Why is it important for trainees to think carefully about lesson content and lesson structure?

CONVERSATIONS WITH PUPILS

Conversations with pupils are not a way of 'spying' on trainees. They are a useful quality assurance strategy which is usually part of a whole school approach to school improvement. Mentors may involve trainees in these meetings as a form of professional development.

Mentors can use these conversations as opportunities to check that pupils have learned the intended curriculum. Pupils can arrive at these meetings with samples of their work. Therefore, mentors can check whether:

+ pupils can talk about the knowledge they have learned;
+ pupils' work demonstrates that they have learned the intended curriculum that the trainee has planned;

+ pupils' work demonstrates that pupils with SEND are accessing the same ambitious curriculum that all pupils have been learning;
+ high standards in presentation are being communicated to pupils.

CRITICAL QUESTIONS

+ What are the advantages of using pupil meetings to inform your assessment of trainees?
+ Are there any disadvantages?

GETTING THE MOST FROM MENTOR MEETINGS

As mentor, you should encourage your trainee to prepare thoroughly for meetings. Be clear about the focus of the meeting, for example by setting meeting agendas. You may wish to ask the trainee to undertake some preparation for the meeting. You might require them to read a specific research paper or to bring some documentary evidence to the meeting. The trainee should not adopt a passive role during meetings. You should require them to reflect on their own development, listen, take notes and ask questions. Be clear about the timescales for meetings, and at the start of meetings it is useful to identify expected outcomes from the meeting. Schedule meetings in advance and set pre-meeting and post-meeting tasks which link to the intended ITE curriculum.

CRITICAL QUESTIONS

+ What other meetings might you ask trainees to participate in, even as a silent observer?
+ Why are regular meetings important and what are the risks if regular meetings do not take place?

TARGET SETTING

Targets are different from actions. An action simply communicates what a trainee needs to do. A target communicates what the trainee needs to improve. Targets may be derived from the ITTECF. Targets may be aligned with actions which combine to enable the trainee to achieve the target. Examples are shown below.

Target: Learn to adapt teaching in a responsive way, including by providing targeted support to pupils who are struggling. (ITTECF, S5.1)

Actions:

1. Identify pupils who would benefit from pre-teaching.

2. Implement pre-teaching in mathematics to enable these pupils to learn the intended curriculum.

3. Design in-class adaptations for these pupils, for example by providing them with worked examples on their desks.

Target: Provide learners with high-quality, clear and accurate feedback which provides specific guidance on how to improve. (ITTECF, S6.5)

Actions:

1. Use the visualiser to share good examples of work in class.

2. Review the example together as a class.

3. Explain to pupils why the work is good.

4. Ask pupils to review their own work against the example that has been shared and to identify areas for improvement in their own work.

CRITICAL QUESTIONS

+ What are the key differences between targets and actions?
+ Use the ITTECF to identify another target and then identify the aligned actions which will support the trainee to achieve the target.

CASE STUDY

ENGAGING TRAINEES IN SELF-ASSESSMENT

At the end of the week, a mentor identified *with the trainee* two or three key targets for the following week. At the end of the following week, the mentor and trainee reviewed the trainee's progress and set new targets. The mentor asked the trainee to bring into each meeting their own self-assessment of their progress against the identified targets. This ensured that the trainee rather than the mentor led the meeting. The mentor asked some *coaching questions* to promote deeper reflection and these questions led to the trainee identifying further actions that they needed to address.

RESEARCH

Unplanned, incidental conversations can have a positive impact on trainees' development (Jones et al, 2019). A dialogic approach to professional conversations is more democratic, but not all mentors are skilled in this approach (Jones et al, 2021).

SUMMARY

This chapter has provided guidance on how to assess trainees' progress. It has covered the range of evidence that you can collate to formulate judgements about trainees' progress and it has addressed target setting.

CHECKLIST

+ Lesson visits, documentary evidence, professional development meetings and meetings with pupils are all possible approaches for assessing trainees' progress.
+ Targets tend to specify what the trainee needs to do to develop their teaching.
+ Multiple actions can underpin a single target.

FURTHER READING

Badia, A and Clarke, A (2022) The Practicum-Mentor Identity in the Teacher Education Context. *Teaching Education*, 33(4): 355–71.

Lofthouse, R M (2018) Re-imagining Mentoring as a Dynamic Hub in the Transformation of Initial Teacher Education: The Role of Mentors and Teacher Educators. *International Journal of Mentoring and Coaching in Education*, 7(3): 248–60.

CHAPTER 8
EDUCATIONAL RESEARCH FOR MENTORS

CHAPTER OBJECTIVES

By the end of this chapter you will understand:

+ the role of educational research in the school-based ITE curriculum;
+ how to support trainees to make connections between educational research and their practice in schools.

INTRODUCTION

Trainee teachers learn about educational research in the centre-based component of the ITE curriculum. The Initial Teacher Training and Early Career Framework (ITTECF) (DfE, 2024a) identifies the pertinent educational research that trainees should learn. Too often, there is a disconnection between what trainees learn in the centre and the practice that they undertake in school. However, there is no reason for this to be the case. Bridging the gap between theory and practice requires trainees to use the best available research evidence to inform the pedagogical approaches that they use in classrooms. If mentors are also informed about the research evidence, they can support trainees to connect the learning they have undertaken in the centre to the pedagogical approaches they are using in classrooms. In addition, improving mentors' knowledge of research can also support whole school improvement.

Schools, their leaders and the educational sector have become increasingly interested in educational research in the last few years. This is evident through the introduction of various initiatives which have facilitated the development of a research-informed teaching profession. One example of this is the introduction of the Chartered College of Teaching led by Professor Dame Alison Peacock. The College publishes research papers and in 2024 it launched its *Research Champions* initiative. Research Champions are educators who build an evidence-informed culture within their own professional contexts. Another initiative is researchEd, which brings together teachers, academics, researchers, policy makers and teacher educators to improve the research literacy of educators. The Research Schools Network works with designated Research Schools to bridge the gap between research and practice. The network is a partnership between the Education Endowment Foundation (EEF) and the Institute for Effective Education (IEE).

WHAT ARE THE CHALLENGES?

Education as a discipline is underpinned by rich research which spans a range of subjects, including, but not limited to, psychology, sociology, history, philosophy and politics. In recent years, the education sector has become increasingly interested in the role of memory in the process of learning and the application of neuroscience to education. However, it is challenging for teachers to find the time to read extensive research papers and many of the existing research papers are hidden behind expensive paywalls. Organisations such as researchEd and the Chartered College of Teaching have produced short summaries of research presented in blogs, short articles and short books to make research more accessible to teachers. The British Educational Research Association has also produced a magazine, a blog site and podcasts for members to make the research easier to access.

Another challenge is to ensure that the trainees and teachers are introduced to research which is current and impactful and has direct relevance to classroom practice. Educational research is an evolving field of enquiry and teachers and academics must keep up to date and be prepared to leave behind dated research and theories which may no longer be relevant to education today. The EEF and the IEE are leading research organisations which focus on producing research which is evidence based and emphasises '*what works*' in educational practice.

It is crucial that trainees do not develop a view that educational research has little relevance to classrooms. University-based ITE programmes are ideally placed to introduce trainee teachers to the latest research evidence. Academics who are responsible for the delivery of centre-based university training must ensure that they keep up to date with the latest research evidence and are also involved in current research projects. This will keep their teaching research informed, which is particularly crucial given that they may not have worked in schools for several years or even for decades. Teacher educators who work in universities and are research active are likely to be at the cutting edge of education. They are practitioners, teachers and researchers who are generating the research that helps to keep the education profession research informed.

CRITICAL QUESTIONS

+ How can mentors bridge the gap between theory and practice?
+ Which type of educational research is valued by the organisations cited above?
+ Which type of research is not valued? Why is this?

CASE STUDY

DEVELOPING A RESEARCH CULTURE IN SCHOOLS

A secondary school appointed Kai to a Head of Research role. Every professional development event included an agenda for research and Kai used these opportunities to share the latest educational research with colleagues. Kai developed a 'teachers as researchers' initiative in the school. Collectively, staff identified some key research themes to focus on. These included assessment, SEND, behaviour, inclusion and teaching strategies. Kai asked staff to align themselves with one of the themes. Staff were then asked to develop a small-scale action research project in their own classrooms to address the theme. Kai supported colleagues to design their projects with the support of researchers

CHAPTER 8: EDUCATIONAL RESEARCH FOR MENTORS

from the local university. Colleagues were asked to implement and evaluate a small-scale intervention. The planning of the research included formulating specific research questions, identifying research methods and determining approaches to support the evaluation of the intervention. The projects ran for one term and the teacher-researchers presented these at a symposium for trainee teachers at the university. Kai developed a website to showcase the projects.

> **RESEARCH**
>
> This section presents summaries of research studies (see Table 8.1). It is not possible within this chapter to cover every research study and therefore we have summarised the best available evidence, drawn from both academic reviews and existing frameworks.

Table 8.1 Summary of educational research

Strand	Summary of findings
Poverty	At the end of primary school, pupils living in poverty are often over nine months behind their peers in reading, writing and maths. Pupils on free school meals for over 80 per cent of their time at school have a learning gap of 22.7 months – twice that of children with a low persistence of poverty (those on free school meals for less than 20 per cent of their time at school), who have a learning gap of 11.3 months (Education Policy Institute, 2020).
Subject knowledge	According to Weston (2020): '**Pedagogical content knowledge** *is the knowledge teachers have of how to teach, explain, model, correct and feedback in their subjects. Shulman (1987) described it as "that special amalgam of content and pedagogy" ... Whilst developing [subject]* **content knowledge** *alone will only have limited returns on student outcomes, developing pedagogical content knowledge has lots of promise. Baumert et al (2010) found that pedagogical content knowledge "makes the greatest contribution to explaining student progress" in*

Table 8.1 (Continued)

Strand	Summary of findings
	investigations comparing with subject content knowledge. Whilst pedagogical content knowledge can't exist without content knowledge, the former is a better predictor of teacher impact than the latter'.
	The Ofsted research reviews are also a useful source of reference for mentors: www.gov.uk/government/collections/curriculum-research-reviews
Memory	To learn, students must transfer information from working memory (where it is consciously processed) to long-term memory (where it can be stored and later retrieved). Students have limited working memory capacities that can be overwhelmed by tasks that are cognitively too demanding. Understanding new ideas can be impeded if students are confronted with too much information at once (Sweller, 1988).
Practice	Practice is essential to learning new facts (Ericsson et al, 1993). Psychological research shows that 'overlearning' (continuing to practise after performance has reached a specified standard) can be important for producing learning that is durable and flexible (Soderstrom et al, 2015). Practice generally needs to be monitored and guided initially (Rosenshine, 2010). For mastery and fluency of subject content, evidence suggests that students need five times more practice than most teachers expect (Engelmann, 1992).
Retrieval	Low- or no-stakes quizzes aid memorisation (Pashler et al, 2007; Agarwal et al, 2012).
	'Retrieval practice describes the process of recalling information from memory with little or minimal prompting. Low stakes tests (such as individual questions or quizzes) are often used as methods of retrieval practice as these require pupils to think hard about what information they have retained and can recall. When used in this way, tests can be a strategy for learning in addition to being an assessment of learning' (EEF, 2021b, p 21).
Spaced practice	Teachers can space practice over time, with content being reviewed across weeks or months, to help

CHAPTER 8: EDUCATIONAL RESEARCH FOR MENTORS

Table 8.1 (Continued)

Strand	Summary of findings
	students remember that content over the long term (Cepeda et al, 2006; Pashler et al, 2007).
Interleaving	Teachers can interleave (ie alternate) practice of different types of content. For example, if students are learning four mathematical operations, it's more effective to interleave practice of different problem types rather than practise just one type of problem, then another type of problem, and so on (Pashler et al, 2007; Rohrer et al, 2015).
Dual coding	*'By presenting content in multiple formats, it is possible that teachers can appeal to both subsystems of the working memory, which subsequently strengthens learning. It is thought that given the specialised nature of the two subsystems of working memory, a larger amount of content can be understood with more richness when conveyed through multiple formats without overloading working memory'* (EEF, 2021b, p 37).
Worked examples	*'There are a large number of studies showing that using worked examples can have a positive impact on learning outcomes'* (EEF, 2021b, p 25).
Synthetic phonics	The evidence for synthetic phonics as an approach to support word reading originated from the Clackmannanshire study (Watson and Johnston, 1998). The research examined the performance of three groups of children who received interventions over a ten-week period. Each intervention lasted for 15 minutes twice a week. One group received sight vocabulary training, the second group received intervention in analytic phonics and the third group received intervention in synthetic phonics. The results led the researchers to conclude that synthetic phonics led to better reading, spelling and phonemic awareness gains than the other two approaches (Watson and Johnston, 1998). Jim Rose in his independent review on the teaching of reading, concluded as follows: *'Having considered a wide range of evidence, the review has concluded that the case for systematic phonic work is overwhelming and much strengthened by a synthetic approach'* (Rose, 2006, p 20, para 51).

→

Table 8.1 (Continued)

Strand	Summary of findings
Simple View of Reading (SVOR)	Gough and Tunmer (1986) developed the Simple View of Reading (SVOR). The model conceptualises reading as the product of word recognition and language comprehension. Skilled readers are proficient in both components. The emphasis in the early stages of reading development is on word recognition, but as pupils become fluent in word recognition there is greater emphasis on language comprehension.
Vocabulary	'Explicit vocabulary teaching strategies have been shown to be effective, both alone and in combination with implicit vocabulary teaching strategies' (EEF, nd).
Reading for pleasure	Reading for pleasure improves educational attainment and attitudes to reading (Clark and De Zoysa, 2011). Providing pupils with choice in relation to reading material, plus incentives and rewards, is important in promoting motivation and healthy reading habits (Clark and Rumbold, 2006).
Schemata	'Schemas (sometimes referred to as mental models, scripts, or frames) are structures that organise knowledge in the mind. When learning, the mind connects new information with pre-existing knowledge, skills, and concepts thereby developing existing schemas' (EEF, 2021b, p 31).
Metacognition	The metacognitive process involves pupils planning, monitoring and evaluating their own learning. Studies involving primary school pupils have typically been more effective (+ eight months' additional progress) than those with secondary school pupils (+ seven months' additional progress) (EEF, 2021c).
Scaffolding	Scaffolding was a concept first introduced by Wood et al (1976), having been influenced by Vygotsky's concept of the *zone of proximal development*. Scaffolding is the process of providing support when pupils are learning new subject content. As pupils become proficient with the content the scaffolding is gradually removed. This is known as fading.

Table 8.1 (Continued)

Strand	Summary of findings
	According to the Education Endowment Foundation: '*Some studies indicated that when fading was used to gradually reduce scaffolding, it was more effective when adapted to the changing knowledge of pupils rather than fading at a fixed rate. One of the risks teachers identified around scaffolding was pupils becoming reliant on the scaffolds. Carefully monitoring pupil expertise and gradually reducing scaffolding might reduce the risk of reliance on scaffolds developing*' (EEF, 2021b, p 28).
Explicit direct teaching	'*Enthusiasm for "discovery learning" is not supported by research evidence, which broadly favours direct instruction (Kirschner et al, 2006). Although learners do need to build new understanding on what they already know, if teachers want them to learn new ideas, knowledge or methods they need to teach them directly*' (Coe et al, 2014, p 23). According to Ashman (2019), '*the principles of explicit teaching directly contradict those of inquiry-based learning*' (p 31). Through enquiry-based approaches students are often required to discover knowledge for themselves or to figure things out. However, the research evidence suggests that enquiry-based learning approaches are less effective than direct teaching (Kirschner et al, 2006) and evidence therefore broadly supports direct instruction (Coe et al, 2014).
Grouping	'*Evidence on the effects of grouping by ability, either by allocating students to different classes, or to within-class groups, suggests that it makes very little difference to learning outcomes (Higgins et al, 2014). Although ability grouping can in theory allow teachers to target a narrower range of pace and content of lessons, it can also create an exaggerated sense of within-group homogeneity and between-group heterogeneity in the teacher's mind*' (Coe et al, 2014, p 23).

→

Table 8.1 (Continued)

Strand	Summary of findings
Promoting thinking	'If you want students to remember something you have to get them to think about it. This might be achieved by being "active" or "passive"' (Coe et al, 2014, p 24). Therefore, students might be listening to the teacher rather than doing an 'activity' but if they are thinking hard, then arguably they are actively engaged in learning.
Explanations	Evidence from both cognitive load theory (Sweller, 1988; Sweller et al, 2019) and direct instruction (Adams and Engelmann, 1996; Stockard et al, 2018) supports the importance of good explanations. These are neither too long, too short, too simple nor too complex.
Questioning	According to Coe et al (2020, p 34): 'Just asking a lot of questions is not a marker of quality; it's about the types of questions, the time allowed for, and depth of, student thinking they provoke or elicit, and how teachers interact with the responses … questioning is a tool to promote deep and connected thinking. Great teachers use questioning as part of a dialogue in which students are engaged and stretched. They prompt students to give explanations and justifications for their answers, or just to improve an initial response, to describe their thinking processes, to elaborate on their answers.'
SEND/adaptive teaching	According to Davis and Florian (2004), there is little evidence to support the use of distinctive teaching approaches for children with specific learning difficulties although responding to individual differences is crucial. In-class differentiation, using different tasks for specific students or different resources, has generally not been shown to have much impact on pupils' attainment (Ofsted, 2019). In Scheerens and Bosker's (1997) meta-analysis of school effectiveness research, differentiation showed a null or a very weak relationship with students' outcomes.

Table 8.1 (Continued)

Strand	Summary of findings
Assessment and feedback	Research shows that feedback can enhance learning powerfully (Hattie and Timperley, 2007). Feedback can help by clarifying or emphasising goals or success criteria (*'Where am I going?'*) (Hattie and Timperley, 2007), thus directing students' attention to productive future goals. It may draw attention to a gap between actual and desired levels of performance, which may be positive if goals are challenging, accepted and accompanied by feelings of self-efficacy (Locke and Latham, 2002).
Behaviour	According to the Education Endowment Foundation: *'Research on Adverse Childhood Experiences demonstrates that being exposed to four or more significant adverse experiences tends to affect children and teenagers' behaviour as well as their physical and mental health, both immediately and throughout their lives ... There is a strong evidence base that teacher-pupil relationships are key to good pupil behaviour and that these relationships can affect pupil effort and academic attainment'* (EEF, 2021d, p 15).
Motivation	Self-determined motivation (a consequence of values or pure interest) leads to better long-term outcomes than controlled motivation (a consequence of reward/punishment or perceptions of self-worth) (Davis et al, 2006). Students will be more motivated and successful in academic environments when they believe that they belong and are accepted in those environments (Yeager et al, 2013).
Self-esteem	Beliefs about intelligence are important predictors of student behaviour in school (Burnette et al, 2013). Self-esteem is a product of *self-worth* (our view of ourselves) and *self-competence* (our ability to master tasks). Overall self-esteem is high when *both* dimensions are also high (Mruk, 1999).

Table 8.1 (Continued)

Strand	Summary of findings
Modelling	Modelling can take various forms. These are summarised below. **Thinking aloud:** This is where teachers explicitly model their thinking by verbalising their thought (Sherrington, 2019). **Worked examples:** More effective teachers '*provide students with many worked examples so that the general patterns are clear, providing a strong basis from which to learn*' (Sherrington, 2019, p 21). **Practical demonstrations:** This is where teachers might model how to complete a specific practical task. **Modelling using student work:** Sharing good examples of students' work with the class and analysing them. Rosenshine's (2010, 2012) principles of instruction include modelling as an example of an effective teaching strategy. Creemers and Kyriakides' (2006, 2011) dynamic model of teaching also includes modelling as a key component of effective teaching.
Frameworks to support teaching	Rosenshine (2010, 2012) developed ten principles of effective instruction. These are summarised below: 1. Begin a lesson with a short review of previous learning. 2. Present new material in small steps, with student practice after each step. 3. Ask many questions and check the responses of all students. 4. Provide models for problem solving and worked examples. 5. Guide student practice. 6. Check for student understanding. 7. Obtain a high success rate. 8. Provide scaffolds for difficult tasks. 9. Require and monitor independent practice. 10. Engage students in weekly and monthly review.

CASE STUDY

DEVELOPING TRAINEES' SUBJECT KNOWLEDGE

You are mentoring a trainee who has very strong content knowledge in science. She provides pupils with accurate explanations and facts. Despite this, the pupils are not engaged in lessons. They quickly become disengaged and there are signs of low-level disruption because the trainee does not provide opportunities for the pupils to work as scientists. The trainee has given insufficient attention to pedagogical content knowledge and disciplinary knowledge. In a mentoring session, you draw on Shulman's definition of pedagogical content knowledge. You also draw on the Ofsted subject report in science to unpack the concept of disciplinary knowledge. You discuss with the trainee ways of embedding disciplinary knowledge into her science lessons. You support the trainee to plan the next lesson, focusing the trainee on pedagogical content knowledge and disciplinary knowledge. You observe the lesson. The pupils are engaged in the learning throughout.

CRITICAL QUESTIONS

+ How important is research to the teaching profession?
+ Research is highly valued in the field of medicine but less valued in education. Why do you think this is?
+ In the case study above, what other mentoring strategies might you have used with this trainee?

SUMMARY

This chapter has summarised some research studies and theoretical models which underpin teaching. It is not possible within the scope of a chapter to cover all the research which mentors need to know. The bibliography at the end of the ITTECF (DfE, 2024a) lists some key studies which mentors might want to read, particularly if they want to deepen their knowledge of how to support trainees to develop a specific area of their practice. It is not necessary to read all the studies that are listed. The 'Further reading' section at the end of this chapter provides some useful organisations which provide research summaries. ITE providers might also wish to provide useful summaries of key research to mentors through blogs, research bites or podcasts. Mentors do not have the time to read lengthy research papers so providers should develop approaches which facilitate quick access to the most pertinent research. Posters, very short videos and embedding research into mentor training are useful ways of supporting the development of research-informed mentoring.

CHECKLIST

+ Mentors need to know the research evidence which underpins effective teaching.
+ Research-informed mentors can implement research-informed mentoring.
+ Research-informed mentoring in schools can bridge the gap between theory and practice.
+ When mentors know the research that underpins teaching, they can provide a stronger rationale for the use of specific pedagogical approaches.

FURTHER READING

The following are useful websites which house summaries of educational research.

British Educational Research Association (BERA) (nd) BERA Blog. [online] Available at: www.bera.ac.uk/blog (accessed 28 March 2024).

Chartered College of Teaching (nd) News and Blogs. [online] Available at: https://chartered.college/news-blogs (accessed 28 March 2024).

Education Endowment Foundation (nd) Teaching and Learning Toolkit: An Accessible Summary of Education Evidence. [online] Available at: https://educationendowmentfoundation.org.uk/education-evidence/teaching-learning-toolkit (accessed 28 March 2024).

Education Endowment Foundation (nd) Blog. [online] Available at: https://educationendowmentfoundation.org.uk/news/blog (accessed 28 March 2024).

Evidence-based Education (nd) Our Blog. [online] Available at: https://evidencebased.education/our-blog (accessed 28 March 2024).

Education Endowment Foundation (2018) Making Best Use of Teaching Assistants: Maximise the Impact of Teaching Assistants. [online] Available at: https://educationendowmentfoundation.org.uk/education-evidence/guidance-reports/teaching-assistants (accessed 28 March 2024).

Ambition Institute (2023) New Evidence That Modelling Bridges the Theory–Practice Gap. [online] Available at: www.ambition.org.uk/blog/new-evidence-that-modelling-bridges-the-theory-practice-gap (accessed 28 March 2024).

CHAPTER 9
SUPPORTING TRAINEES' WORKLOAD AND MENTAL HEALTH

CHAPTER OBJECTIVES

By the end of this chapter you will understand:

+ the factors that affect trainee workload and mental health;
+ strategies to support trainees to manage their workload and their mental health;
+ strategies to support your own mental health as a mentor.

INTRODUCTION

In recent years, the Department for Education and Ofsted in England have become increasingly concerned about the workload and well-being of trainee teachers and serving teachers. Both aspects have been embedded into the current inspection frameworks for schools and ITE providers. This chapter outlines some of the key issues and presents some approaches for addressing workload and well-being issues. These policy developments must be considered in relation to increasing concerns about job satisfaction, teacher burnout and attrition from the teaching profession. Workload and well-being are related in that high workloads can impact detrimentally on well-being. However, positive well-being is also shaped by school cultures in which teachers have agency, are valued and respected, and are trusted to do their jobs to the best of their abilities. Therefore, addressing workload in itself is not enough on its own to address teachers' well-being. This chapter also presents some theoretical models which underpin mental health and well-being.

FACTORS AFFECTING TRAINEES' WORKLOAD AND MENTAL HEALTH

Research highlights that early career teachers (ECTs) in England experience significant well-being issues (Jerrim et al, 2020). This is unsurprising given that research also indicates that teachers generally experience stress, burnout and mental fatigue (McLean et al, 2019). It is also concerning that internationally, between a third and a half of teachers leave teaching within the first five years (Skaalvik and Skaalvik, 2016).

Frequent policy changes, including changes to the curriculum and assessments (DfE, 2018), funding cuts (Ball, 2021) and significant changes in pupil demographics (DfE, 2022) all adversely impact teacher well-being. For trainees, relationships with other colleagues and pupils are critically important in maintaining and developing resilience over time. Greenfield's model (Greenfield, 2015) identifies some of the key factors which affect teachers' resilience. An adapted model is shown in Figure 9.1.

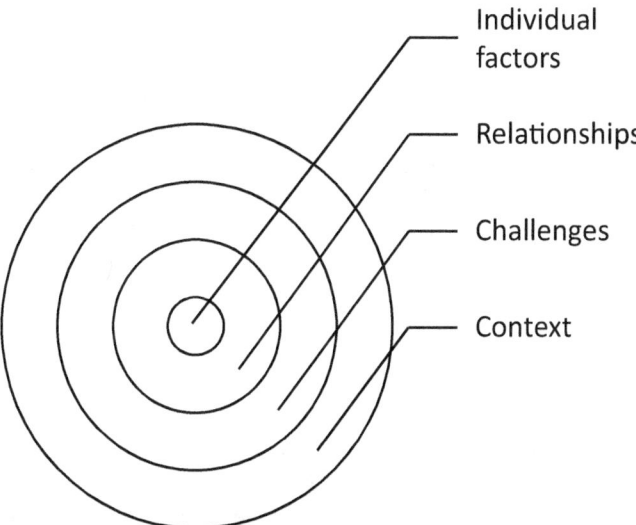

Figure 9.1 Adapted model of teacher resilience (Greenfield, 2015)

CRITICAL QUESTIONS

+ How might you use this model with trainees?
+ What challenges in school might adversely influence trainees' resilience and well-being?
+ What context-related factors in school might adversely influence trainees' resilience and well-being?

INDIVIDUAL FACTORS

Individual factors can influence resilience. These include a sense of hope and purpose and self-efficacy. Trainees will experience several challenges in classrooms and schools. If they are intrinsically motivated to be a teacher, this will help them to stay resilient when they experience challenges in the role. Intrinsic motivation may derive from a determination to influences pupils' life chances, a belief in the power of education to influence lives and shape attitudes, and a belief that teaching is interesting, exciting and richly rewarding. Trainees who are extrinsically motivated may be motivated by salary, possible future promotion and the misguided belief that they will get many holidays. These trainees may be less resilient when they experience challenges, and they may have poor well-being because they may not gain satisfaction from doing the job.

Self-efficacy relates to competence. Trainees with high self-efficacy are likely to be competent in the roles they are required to undertake in schools and classrooms. Trainees with low self-efficacy are likely to find aspects of being a teacher challenging. The mentor plays a crucial role in developing trainees' self-efficacy through using a variety of mentoring approaches. Skilled mentors can *model* effective teaching approaches. They can undertake lesson visits with trainees and use the technique of *deconstruction* to isolate specific aspects of teaching that they want the trainee to focus on. They can use *instructional coaching* by setting targets with trainees and supporting trainees to break these targets down into smaller milestones. They can support trainees to reflect regularly on their own teaching to help them to improve. They can provide trainees with *developmental feedback* on their teaching so that trainees know what they are doing well and what they need to improve. These mentoring approaches will improve self-efficacy, which will improve trainees' self-esteem, resilience and well-being.

RELATIONSHIPS

Positive relationships with mentors and other colleagues in school, as well as positive relationships with pupils, help to support trainees' resilience and well-being. Mentors should spend some time getting to know the trainee and establishing a professional and supportive relationship, much like they do with their own pupils when they are teaching. Trainees are more likely to thrive if they establish positive relationships with their mentor.

CRITICAL QUESTIONS

+ What factors might negatively impact on trainee–mentor relationships?
+ What can mentors do to establish positive relationships with trainees?
+ What can trainees do to establish positive relationships with their mentors?

The relationship between a mentor and a trainee is not a one-way relationship. Trainees also need to invest in developing that relationship. They share an equal responsibility for establishing professional and positive relationships with their mentors.

One useful strategy is for mentors to set out an informal contract with trainees at the start of a placement. Mentors should communicate their expectations clearly to trainees and particularly the professional boundaries which should exist. Trainees sometimes assume that they can contact their mentor outside of work at unsociable times. It is important that mentors communicate clearly from the outset any deadlines which the trainee needs to meet and the times that they are both available and unavailable.

Weekly mentor meetings should be scheduled from the start of a placement, and specific tasks which the mentor expects the trainee to undertake, and by when, should be clearly communicated. The mentor should spend time introducing the trainee to key colleagues, codes of conduct and key policies, and they should provide the trainee with a teaching timetable. These simple actions enable mentors to manage the relationship with their trainee. These actions also alleviate anxiety for trainees, particularly those trainees who need to know exactly what is required of them.

Positive relationships also rely on approachability. Effective mentors make themselves available, they work with the trainee to secure positive outcomes, they celebrate the trainee's successes with them, and they support trainees when they experience challenges. These approaches will directly impact positively on trainees' well-being. When relationships are both professional and supportive, it is easier for mentors to provide trainees with critical but developmental feedback on their teaching. If the relationship is too informal, the mentor might find it difficult to talk to the trainee about aspects of their teaching that they need to improve. If the relationship is too hierarchical, trainees may be reluctant to talk to their mentors when they are finding something challenging.

CRITICAL QUESTIONS

+ One of the challenges of mentoring is that the role of the mentor is a dual role. Mentors have responsibility for both *developing* and *assessing* trainees' teaching practice. What issues can this create in the mentor–mentee relationship?
+ When might a mentor need to provide more challenge than support?
+ When might a mentor need to provide more support than challenge?

CHALLENGES

Teaching and challenges go together. You cannot have one without the other. Trainees can experience a range of challenges, which may include:

+ lessons not going to plan;
+ pupils' demonstrating low-level disruption in the trainee's lesson or more challenging behaviours;
+ periods of heavy workload and managing multiple tasks;
+ long travel times to get to school;
+ trainees having to undertake paid work outside of placements to enable them to manage financially;
+ complaints from parents;

- concerns being raised from other colleagues about the trainee;
- trainees experiencing anxiety when they are about to teach a lesson;
- trainees experiencing exhaustion;
- personal challenges which trainees might be experiencing, including relationship breakdowns.

CRITICAL QUESTIONS

- What other challenges might trainees experience?
- Choose some of the above challenges. As a mentor, how might you support trainees with these challenges?

Challenges can adversely affect well-being and resilience. Most individuals thrive on some challenge in their lives but when the challenges feel too great, this can impact on overall self-esteem. Avoiding specific challenges is also not helpful because trainees need to learn how to address these to grow as a teacher and it is quite likely that they will experience the same challenges in different schools with various classes and in other situations. The mentor plays a crucial role in talking through situations and scenarios with trainees and in empowering trainees to respond to specific challenges.

When trainees approach a mentor to discuss a specific challenge that they are experiencing, mentors might find the following framework, LATER, helpful.

- **L**isten to the trainee.
- **A**cknowledge what they are telling you.
- **T**alk with them, not at them.
- **E**mpathise.
- **R**eview together what needs to happen next (actions for the trainee and actions for the mentor).

CRITICAL QUESTIONS

- If a trainee is experiencing challenges but they do not say anything to you, how would you identify this?
- What would you do if you notice that the trainee is finding something challenging but they do not want to admit this to you?

CONTEXT

The school context can affect a trainee's resilience and well-being. If there is a positive school culture which promotes a sense of belonging, trainees can thrive. Specific school contexts can also influence trainees' well-being and resilience. Some trainees might find it more difficult to thrive in a school where there are many disadvantaged pupils or a large volume of pupils with special educational needs. Some trainees might find it difficult to work in a faith school. Some may struggle to thrive in a school where there are significant numbers of pupils whose first language is not English. Others may struggle in a large urban school with pupils from diverse backgrounds and some may find it challenging to work in small rural schools with mixed-aged classes.

Regardless of what trainees perceive to be a challenge, it is critically important that all trainees have experience of working in schools with a variety of contexts. Sometimes trainees might find it difficult to work in a context that they are not used to, but regardless of this, trainees do need to learn how to work with a variety of pupils with diverse needs and backgrounds. The skill of a mentor is to *scaffold* the whole experience so that the trainee gradually develops their confidence.

The wider policy context can also influence trainees' well-being and resilience. At the end of their training, they are required to meet the Teachers' Standards. This performative aspect of teacher training can cause stress for some trainees, particularly if there are specific standards that they are still yet to meet. The mentors can scaffold their development by breaking tasks down into smaller steps and provide feedback on their development after each step to help them to achieve specific standards.

SUPPORTING TRAINEES TO FLOURISH

Self-determination theory (Deci and Ryan, 1985) outlines the key factors which support human beings to flourish. These are shown in Figure 9.2.

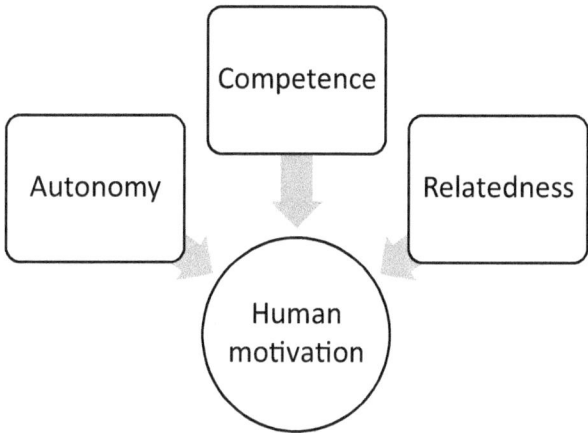

Figure 9.2 Theory of human motivation
(Deci and Ryan, 1985)

CRITICAL QUESTIONS

+ Human beings are more motivated when they experience autonomy. How can you facilitate this as a mentor?

+ Competence is a key factor in human motivation. Developing a skill to automaticity through repeated practice is one way of developing competence. How can you support trainees to develop automaticity in their teaching?

+ Relatedness includes developing effective connections with people and organisations. How might you facilitate this as a mentor?

TRAINEES' SELF-ESTEEM

Mruk's model of self-esteem demonstrates that our overall self-esteem is made up of self-worth (our view of ourselves) and self-competence (how well we complete challenges and tasks). This is shown in Figure 9.3.

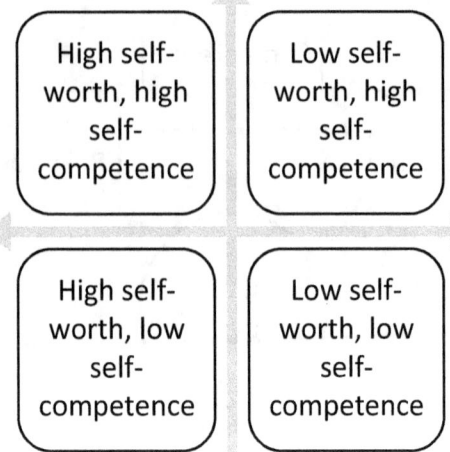

Figure 9.3 Two-dimensional model of self-esteem
(Adapted from Mruk, 1999)

The vertical axis represents self-worth, and the horizontal axis represents self-competence. To achieve overall high self-esteem, individuals need to have both high self-worth and high self-competence. Where there is a mismatch between self-worth and self-competence, this results in defensive self-esteem and individuals in these two quadrants can demonstrate signs of poor mental health. Individuals who are low in both dimensions (self-worth and self-competence) are also at risk of developing mental ill-health.

CRITICAL QUESTIONS

+ What factors might result in a trainee having low self-worth?
+ What factors might result in a trainee having high self-worth and low self-competence?
+ What actions might you implement to move a trainee from defensive self-esteem to high self-esteem?

STRATEGIES TO SUPPORT TRAINEES TO MANAGE THEIR OWN WELL-BEING AND MENTAL HEALTH

Our well-being is unbalanced if we do not have the resources to counteract the challenges that we experience. This can be represented as a see-saw (see Figure 9.4). If the challenges are too great but the resources are not sufficient to meet these challenges, the see-saw is not balanced.

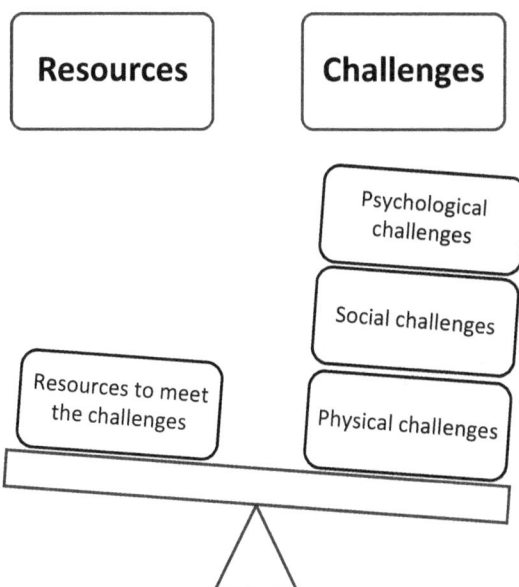

Figure 9.4 The well-being see-saw
(Adapted from Dodge et al, 2012)

CRITICAL QUESTIONS

+ How might you use this model with trainees?
+ What psychological, physical or social challenges might trainees experience?
+ What resources might trainees draw on to counteract the challenges?

MANAGING STRESS

Stress can result in anxiety and other mental health conditions. The model of the stress container is a useful visual representation to demonstrate the capacity of human beings to cope with stress. Everyone has the capacity to manage stress, although this capacity varies across individuals. When the container becomes full, we cannot accommodate any more stress and the container starts to overflow. We might demonstrate specific behaviours when this occurs, including becoming upset, angry or withdrawn. The solution is to release some of the stress to create capacity in the container. The stress container is shown in Figure 9.5 and it can be used with trainees to help them to understand (a) their own stress capacity and (b) what actions they can take to reduce the stress in their stress container.

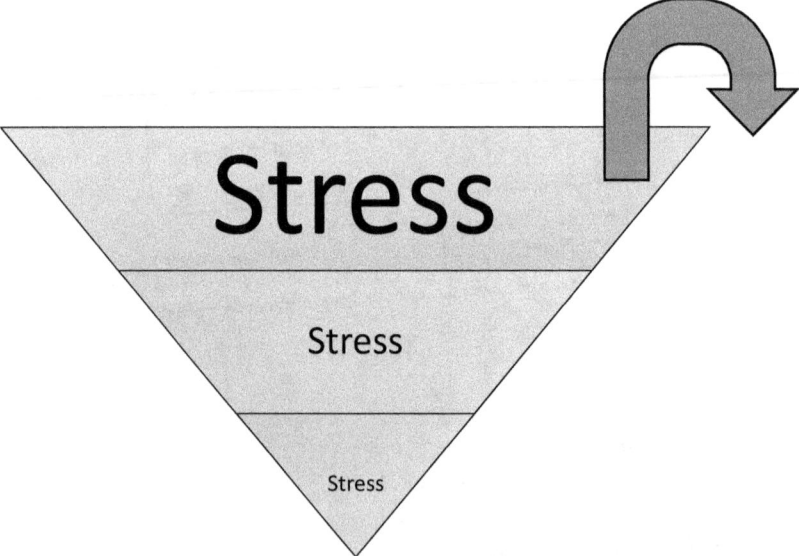

Figure 9.5 Visual representation: stress container

MANAGING WORKLOAD

Trainees need to learn how to manage multiple tasks at the same time and they need to learn how to prioritise tasks. Mentors can discuss

CHAPTER 9: SUPPORTING TRAINEES' WORKLOAD AND MENTAL HEALTH

with the trainee how they manage their own workloads, including the strategies that they find beneficial and the strategies which are less helpful. Trainees might find it beneficial to maintain a list of daily tasks that they need to complete, and they can get into the habit of organising these tasks into order of priority. Trainees may also need guidance on the time limits for completing specific tasks. Some trainees are perfectionists and will spend many hours planning a single lesson. However, this is not a realistic investment of time, and it will result in other tasks being unfinished or not even started. Trainees need to learn early in their training not to invest significant time into making a resource that they will only use once. Mentors can support them to use resources which have already been produced and are available to use or to adapt resources which other people have produced. Many schools will already have banks of lesson plans and resources for everyone to use and schools may be following specific schemes of work in some subjects. Mentors can support trainees to evaluate what is already available and make suggestions for adapting resources to meet the needs of the class(es) that the trainee is teaching. In addition, mentors should discuss with trainees how to maximise their time in school, for example by marking work in class, providing pupils with live feedback in lessons, and the use of agreed codes and symbols to make marking more efficient.

Figure 9.6 is a useful task to carry out with trainees to support them to think about prioritisation of tasks.

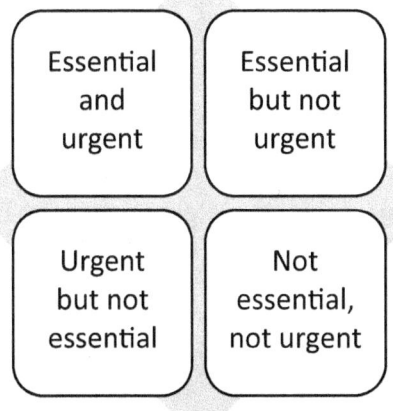

Figure 9.6 Task prioritisation

The mentors could develop scenarios for trainees to consider. Trainees could place each scenario into the appropriate category. Safeguarding concerns will always be categorised as 'essential and urgent'.

CRITICAL QUESTIONS

+ What tasks in teaching are essential and urgent?
+ What tasks are essential but not urgent?
+ What tasks are not essential and not urgent?
+ Can any tasks fit in the bottom left quadrant? If something is urgent, can it also be classed as 'non-essential'?

CASE STUDY

SUPPORTING A NON-BINARY TRAINEE

Ned is a non-binary trainee and uses they/them pronouns. The mentor had completed training on equality, diversity and inclusion and was therefore able to facilitate an inclusive induction into the school. Ned had already written a letter of introduction to the school prior to attending on the first day. The mentor met with Ned to discuss the school's policy on inclusion. They agreed that the pupils could use Ned's first name rather than using 'Mx'. Ned was worried that the pupils might ask them questions about their gender. The mentor and Ned talked through possible questions that the pupils might ask. Together, the mentor and Ned formulated a suitable response should the pupils ask any questions. Ned was also worried that they might encounter discriminatory behaviour from pupils or other staff in school. The mentor reassured Ned that this would be taken seriously should it arise, and they informed Ned how to report any discrimination. This meeting was critical for Ned because it alleviated so much anxiety.

LOOKING AFTER YOUR OWN WELL-BEING

It is important that you manage your own well-being as a mentor. It is likely that you also have senior or middle leadership responsibilities on top of your mentoring role. The following suggestions may be useful:

+ Agree with trainees any deadlines for submitting work to you.
+ Communicate to trainees when you will be available for them and when you will not be available.
+ Model professional working arrangements: explain to trainees that your time outside school is protected. Explain that you will not respond to messages at unsociable hours and that communications should take place during the normal working day. Explain that you have other commitments to the school on top of your mentoring responsibilities.
+ If trainees are exhibiting signs of poor mental health, then it is appropriate to listen to them, show empathy and agree solutions. However, it is important to remember that you are not a mental health professional. In some instances, it is appropriate to refer them back to the ITT provider. ITT providers have their own services for supporting well-being.
+ Schedule meetings with trainees as early as possible during the working day.
+ Try not to schedule meetings with trainees at the end of the day. Scheduling during the day helps to keep the meeting to a specified time because you will have commitments before and after the meeting with the trainee.
+ Try to be approachable but maintain professional boundaries. You are not required to give trainees your personal contact details. You can specify if you wish all communications to come through school systems during the working day.
+ Do not make the paperwork onerous: write up lesson observation reports during the lesson. Write the report of the weekly mentor meeting with trainees during the lesson. Remember that the quality of the reports is more important than the length of them. Writing reports 'in the moment' is a way of modelling efficient working practices to trainees.

+ When providing trainees with feedback, give them the 'headlines' and limit the time for this meeting. It is not necessary to deconstruct lessons minute by minute. It is more important to provide trainees with pertinent points that will impact on future teaching practice.
+ During interim progress meetings or final assessments, write up the reports during the meeting.
+ Require trainees to demonstrate independence: you do not have to do everything for them.

CRITICAL QUESTIONS

+ What other things might you do to support your well-being when undertaking the mentoring role?
+ What challenges might you experience when mentoring trainees which might adversely impact on your well-being and how might you address these?

CASE STUDY

MANAGING TRAINEES' EXPECTATIONS

Ameena was a mentor for Alex who was a trainee in a secondary school. Ameena initially met with Alex and went through the school's code of conduct for staff. Ameena explained to Alex that she needed to see her lesson plans at the end of each week for the following week's teaching. She gave Alex her personal mobile number but asked her only to use it in case of emergencies. At first, the placement ran smoothly. After three weeks the workload for Alex increased in line with an increased teaching commitment. Alex started texting Ameena at 10pm in the evenings, requesting help with lesson planning. She missed the deadline for submitting planning and Alex started sending planning to Ameena at 11.30pm on Sunday night. Ameena could not review the plans before Monday because she was asleep.

After two weeks, Ameena requested a meeting with Alex. Ameena explained that she had some concerns relating to Alex's organisation, but more importantly her mental health and well-being. Ameena reiterated that she wanted to support Alex. Alex 'opened up' to Ameena and told her that she also had a part-time job in a bar, which she did in the evenings and at weekends and this was the reason for her lack of organisation. Although both Alex and Ameena would have preferred for Alex not to work in a bar, the cost-of-living crisis meant that she needed to work to pay for her rent, food and bills. Together, Ameena and Alex developed a strategy to address the issue. Alex was given one additional hour per day to dedicate to lesson planning, but Alex had to agree to submitting the plans to Ameena on Friday for the following week's teaching. This was not an ideal solution, but it did mean that Alex could successfully complete her ITT phase.

RESEARCH

Gillett-Swan and Grant-Smith (2020) investigated mentor well-being during placements. They found that the mentoring role was stressful, in part due to the compressed nature of placements. Mentors were concerned about the well-being of trainees, but these concerns also had an adverse impact on mentors' own mental health and well-being. Mentors also did not always feel that they could 'push back' against the expectations of the provider, which they believed did not always serve in the best interests of their trainees. The researchers recommended that ITE providers should consider implementing mental health first aid training to mentors so that mentors can provide immediate support and triage and know when to make a referral for specialist mental health support. The researchers also suggested the use of a mentoring team within schools to support a trainee, so that a single mentor does not have total responsibility for mentoring. This 'team approach' to mentoring would distribute the responsibility for mentoring to other colleagues and support mentors' well-being. However, there are financial and practical/logistical implications of this model which would need consideration.

SUMMARY

Trainees cannot thrive if their well-being and resilience are adversely affected. Resilience operates within a socio-ecological framework. Access to a supportive mentor and other colleagues in school can make a significant difference to a trainee's well-being. However, mentors also need to consider the impact of mentoring on their own well-being. The suggestions in this chapter may support mentors to manage trainee expectations, which should, in turn, support their own well-being.

CHECKLIST

+ Well-being and resilience are closely connected.
+ Mentors can improve trainees' self-efficacy through specific approaches, including coaching, deconstruction and modelling of pedagogical approaches.
+ Supportive school contexts support trainees' well-being and resilience.
+ Access to supportive colleagues also supports well-being and resilience.
+ Mentors can support trainees to develop skills in task prioritisation.

FURTHER READING

Education Support is a national charity which offers a free helpline and support service to teachers. Further details can be found here: www.educationsupport.org.uk (accessed 28 March 2024).

CHAPTER 10
MENTORING EARLY CAREER TEACHERS

> **CHAPTER OBJECTIVES**
>
> **By the end of this chapter you will understand:**
> + the roles and responsibilities of different stakeholders;
> + how to address key professional challenges.

INTRODUCTION

The original Early Career Framework (ECF) (DfE, 2019b) for new teachers in England stated that:

Teachers are the foundation of the education system – there are no great schools without great teachers. Teachers deserve high quality support throughout their careers, particularly in those first years of teaching when the learning curve is steepest.

(DfE, 2019b, p 4)

The purpose of the ECF was to provide early career teachers (ECTs) with a structured induction and to revisit and deepen components of the ITE curriculum. The Framework has now been subsumed into the ITTECF (DfE, 2024a). The Initial Teacher Training and Early Career Framework (ITTECF) states that:

The ITTECF sets out the entitlement of every trainee and early career teacher (ECT) to the core body of knowledge, skills and behaviours that define great teaching, and to the mentoring and support from expert colleagues they should receive throughout the three or more years at the start of their career. ECTs will purposefully revisit the elements of teaching introduced in ITT to deepen their knowledge and understanding. The ITTECF remains designed to equip all trainees and ECTs with a shared body of knowledge and skills, irrespective of subject or phase.

(DfE, 2024a, p 4)

It is not a curriculum and is not designed as an assessment framework. ECTs should continue to be assessed against the Teachers' Standards and Qualified Teacher Status is confirmed at the end of the two-year phase. The new Framework includes significantly more content related to adaptive teaching and supporting pupils with SEND in response to the challenging contexts which schools in England are facing. The Framework is flexible in that it can be adapted to suit different contexts. For example, the statement '*requiring high quality oral language*' within section 3 of the Framework may have less relevance if trainees are working in special schools with pupils with language and communication impairments or complex disabilities. This chapter outlines some of the responsibilities of key stakeholders and it addresses some of the challenges that mentors and induction tutors might experience.

CRITICAL QUESTIONS

+ Do you agree with a single framework to support the ITT and ECF phases? Explain your answer.
+ What are the arguments for and against a single framework?

ECTs' MINIMUM ENTITLEMENT

ECTs are entitled to receive a programme of training, a reduced timetable and ongoing mentoring from a mentor. In addition, they are entitled to scheduled progress reviews and assessment meetings with the induction tutor.

THE ROLE OF THE APPROPRIATE BODY

Appropriate bodies can include local authorities, teaching school hubs or other organisations which have been approved by the Department for Education. The appropriate body makes the final decision as to whether an ECT's performance against the Teachers' Standards is satisfactory, drawing on the recommendation of the headteacher/principal. The appropriate body should also monitor the return of progress review outcomes from progress meetings and assessment reports from assessment meetings, contacting schools if these have not been sent.

THE ROLE OF DELIVERY PARTNERS

Schools can work with approved accredited providers who are responsible for designing and delivering training materials. Schools can also choose to deliver their own training using Department for Education accredited materials or by designing their own training materials which address the full scope of the ITTECF.

THE ROLE OF THE INDUCTION TUTOR

Headteachers or principals must identify an induction tutor. The induction tutor provides regular monitoring and support and assesses the ECT against the Teachers' Standards. The induction tutor must have Qualified Teacher Status. They are responsible for co-ordinating early support and intervention in cases where ECTs are not making adequate progress. The induction tutor is required to undertake scheduled progress reviews with the ECT each term. These are not formal assessments and ECTs are not required to collate evidence in a folder to support the discussions that take place in these meetings. The induction tutor should also schedule formal assessment meetings and keep written records of all meetings. They should arrange a final assessment meeting at the end of the induction period. The induction tutor should keep the ECT informed about their progress. Information provided at assessment points should not come as a surprise to the ECT. In some circumstances it may be necessary for the induction tutor to instigate capability procedures before the end of the induction period if progress is not satisfactory. This could lead to dismissal before the end of the induction period.

CRITICAL QUESTIONS

+ What are the potential challenges associated with the role of the induction tutor?
+ How might these be overcome?

THE ROLE OF THE ECT MENTOR

The role of the mentor is different to the role of the induction tutor. Mentors are responsible for providing coaching and development and for scheduling regular meetings with the ECT. Mentors may review training materials with the ECT, provide training and development, and undertake lesson visits which are designed to be developmental, and they may model pedagogical approaches. They may arrange training experiences, including arranging meetings with other colleagues to support the ECT's development, arrange visits to other schools and review educational research.

CRITICAL QUESTIONS

+ What approaches to mentoring might the mentor use?
+ How will you ensure that ECTs do not simply repeat what they learned during the ITT phase?
+ Choose one or two '*Learn that*' or '*Learn how to*' statements from the ITTECF. How might you ensure that these are related to the context of the school?

CASE STUDY

ADAPTIVE TEACHING

Following a training session with the delivery partner of adaptive teaching, the mentor arranged a follow-up meeting with the ECT to discuss pupils with SEND in the school. The mentor shared the school SEND policy and the approach for identifying pupils with SEND. The mentor then asked the ECT to identify pupils with SEND in their class(es). They discussed the needs of specific pupils and they identified whether the pupils had an education, health and care plan or were on SEND support. The mentor then discussed interventions to support pupils with specific needs that were being implemented throughout the school. The mentor arranged for the ECT to 'shadow' staff who were responsible for the implementation of these interventions. This was timetabled during the ECT's professional development time, across several sessions. The mentor arranged a follow-up meeting and asked the ECT to reflect on what they had learned, with specific emphasis on what approaches the ECT intended to use in their own classroom(s).

THE ROLES AND RESPONSIBILITIES OF ECTs

Teachers cannot be employed in schools in England unless they have satisfactorily completed a statutory induction period. There is no set time for completing the induction. If teachers intend to work *solely* in the independent sector, a free school, an academy, an independent nursery or a further education institution there is no legal requirement to complete an induction, although organisations may insist that they must. An ECT only has one chance to complete the induction. If they fail to meet the Teachers' Standards by the end of the induction period, they are not permitted to repeat the induction. In these circumstances, they will not lose their Qualified Teacher Status, but they will not be allowed to work in a relevant school as a teacher. Induction cannot be served in a secure training centre or a school in special measures where Ofsted have identified that the school is not permitted to induct ECTs. The list of relevant schools where induction can take place is listed in the original Framework.

ECTs are required to engage with the induction process. They must attend scheduled training sessions, engage with the training materials and complete any associated tasks which are required. ECTs are responsible for evaluating their own progress, identifying development needs and taking action to improve their teaching practice. They must engage with the mentoring process fully and co-operate with both the mentor and the induction tutor.

APPROACHES TO MENTORING

Some research suggests that instructional coaching can be limiting and deprofessionalising (Daly et al, 2022; Platt, 2022), but many of the approved delivery partners are committed to this approach (Spicksley and Kington, 2024). Effective mentors do not just provide coaching. They motivate teachers and foster self-efficacy (Vangrieken et al, 2015). They establish positive relationships with their mentees (Spicksley and Watkins, 2020) and collegiality (Spicksley and Kington, 2024). They focus on shaping values to support the development of a strong teacher identity. To be effective, mentoring should be supportive, individualised, developmental, empowering and non-evaluative/non-judgemental. It is likely that mentors will need to draw on different approaches to meet the needs of the teachers they are supporting and, therefore, one size may not fit all.

Regardless of the approach(es) used, mentors are likely to draw on a combination of the following mentoring strategies:

+ **Agree goals/targets.** ECTs should be involved in this process so that they have ownership of their professional development.
+ **Modelling.** Explicit modelling of specific pedagogical approaches by the mentor.
+ **Mentoring conversations.** Regular dialogue to support values and identity development and reflection on the ECT's teaching practice.
+ **Lesson visits.** Observations of the ECT's teaching practice and guided observations of other teachers.
+ **Deconstruction.** Following lesson visits, mentors might isolate specific aspects of pedagogy to focus the ECT's attention on those.
+ **Reviewing training materials.** ECT mentors play a crucial role in contextualising the training materials to the school. For example, following a training session on SEND, mentors might discuss with ECTs the pedagogical approaches used in the school to support pupils with SEND or the approaches to identification, assessment, interventions and review.
+ **Guided/supported lesson planning and assessment.** Mentors might support ECTs with aspects of lesson planning or assessment (including marking, feedback and moderation) and gradually reduce the support as their competence increases. This is known as scaffolding and fading.

+ **Co-teaching.** Mentors and ECTs might co-plan and co-teach a lesson and then jointly reflect on this process afterwards.
+ **Arranging meetings with experts.** Mentors might arrange for ECTs to meet with subject leaders, the SENCO, the designated safeguarding lead and other staff with significant whole school responsibilities. These meetings will have a specific purpose. The mentor might also arrange for ECTs to visit other schools or to 'shadow' colleagues.
+ **Arranging external professional development.** Mentors might arrange for ECTs to participate in local continuing professional development (CPD) or attend network events.

CRITICAL QUESTIONS

+ What other mentoring approaches could be used that are not listed above?
+ What do you think are the attributes of an effective ECT mentor?
+ How might mentoring an ECT be different to ITT mentoring? What might you do with an ECT that you would not do with an ITT trainee?

BUILDING ON THE ITE CURRICULUM

The purpose of the ECF phase is to deepen knowledge that has been learned in the ITE phase. The ECF should also provide rich opportunities for ECTs to apply that knowledge to the professional context in which they are working. The '*Learn that*' and '*Learn how to*' statements are identical for both the ITT and ECT phases. However, it is important that delivery partners and mentors do not simply repeat content which ECTs have already learned. A recent evaluation of the implementation of the ECF identified the following issues:

+ *ECTs were frustrated about the lack of tailoring curriculum content to the school context and learner needs.*
+ *ECTs felt that content was repeated from the ITT phase. One-third of ECTs felt that their induction didn't expose them to new knowledge.*
+ *ECTs felt that the workload was too high.*

- Mentors were frustrated about a perceived lack of tailoring of their mentor training to their phase of education.
- Mentors felt that mentor training was overly prescriptive, and they perceived a lack of networking opportunities to share experiences and insights.
- ECTs valued their mentors highly.

(DfE, 2024c)

CRITICAL QUESTIONS

- What are the implications of these findings for mentors?
- What do you think is the biggest issue identified above?

Table 10.1 provides some general guidance to support mentors in contextualising the content from the ITTECF.

Table 10.1 Linking the ITTECF to the school context

ITTECF strand	Contextualising the training: Mentors might support ECTs to learn ...
High expectations	School and classroom rules.
	Whole school priorities – school improvement plan.
	Agreed language and behaviours that are part of a whole school approach.
	Strategies for engaging parents.
	How to support specific pupils who live in poverty or have English as an Additional Language (EAL).
How pupils learn	How to design classrooms to reduce distractions.
	How to plan lessons which minimise cognitive load and include retrieval, repetition and deliberate practice.
Subject and curriculum	About curriculum resources, for example, schemes for English, phonics, mathematics, PSHE (personal, social and health education).

Table 10.1 (Continued)

ITTECF strand	Contextualising the training: Mentors might support ECTs to learn ...
	About subject content knowledge and pedagogical content knowledge through discussions with subject leaders. Subject interventions, for example, reading interventions.
Classroom practice	About specific pedagogical approaches through guided planning and guided lesson visits – for example, questioning, explanations, modelling. School homework policy. Grouping arrangements used in classrooms.
Adaptive teaching	The school approach to SEND, for example, meeting the SENCO to discuss the school SEND policy, specific SEND interventions, how to meet pupils' needs through adaptive teaching, record-keeping requirements, SEND review meetings, how to work with parents of pupils with SEND, how to assess pupils' learning and the roles of teaching assistants across the school. The relationship between SEND and safeguarding.
Assessment	How to build formative assessment into lesson planning through guided planning. How teachers identify misconceptions: use of guided lesson visits and deconstruction. Statutory assessments and mark schemes. Phonics screening check. Multiplication tables check. Teacher assessment of pupils' work – for example, writing. Involvement in assessment moderation meetings. How to judge pupils' progress across a range of evidence. The school data system. Assessment, marking and feedback policy. Education, health and care plans and individual education plans.

Table 10.1 (Continued)

ITTECF strand	Contextualising the training: Mentors might support ECTs to learn ...
Managing behaviour	Behaviour policy – for example, rewards and sanctions. Bullying policy and how to respond to bullying. How to manage transitions. How to manage low-level disruption. How to manage challenging behaviour – for example, how to promote self-regulation strategies. Classroom routines. Working with parents Use of 'decompression' spaces. Managing large groups – for example, an assembly.
Professional behaviours	School code of conduct for teachers. Safeguarding responsibilities – meet with safeguarding lead. How to record incidents, and manage disclosures and safeguarding concerns. School electronic system for reporting safeguarding concerns. How to write reports. How to conduct a parents' evening. How to support the wider life of the school. Strategies to support personal organisation, well-being and mental health, workload and resilience. Managing professional relationships and conflict with colleagues.

CRITICAL QUESTIONS

+ What more do you think you could add to Table 10.1?

+ Take one of the strands in the ITTECF and review the examples given. What mentoring approaches might you use to develop ECTs' knowledge of this strand?

+ If you are an ECT mentor in a special school or social, emotional and mental health setting, how might you contextualise the ITTECF to the specific context in which you are working?

ADDRESSING PROFESSIONAL CHALLENGES

One of the key professional challenges that you might experience as an ECT mentor is that the ECT might have weaknesses in specific areas of their practice or is generally weak across a range of Teachers' Standards. One way of addressing this is to target your mentoring on the aspects of their practice that need to be further developed. If pupils are struggling to understand something or master a specific skill, you will be skilled in breaking the content down for them into a series of smaller, more manageable steps. You might support them initially to develop increased mastery of the knowledge or skill (scaffolding). As soon as you notice signs of progress, you might gradually withdraw the support (fading) until they can work independently. You might need to implement specific adaptive strategies so that they have the pivotal foundational knowledge that is essential for learning the subject.

When you are mentoring ECTs who demonstrate specific weaknesses, it might be beneficial to model pedagogical approaches which they are trying to master. Consider the following reflective questions:

+ How can I break this down into smaller steps so that it is more manageable?

+ What modelling do I need to provide?

+ What guided support can I provide, for example in planning, in teaching or through conducting lesson visits?

+ How might I use deconstruction as a key mentoring approach?

- What additional literature or resources might I provide to support the ECT?
- When is it appropriate to gradually fade out the scaffolding?
- Which other experts in the school or multi-academy trust can support the ECT?

If it is unlikely that the ECT will meet the Teachers' Standards by the end of the statutory induction period, the induction tutor should have communicated this with the ECT so that the information does not come as a surprise. The decision to fail an ECT is significant, given the investment in resources to support them through their initial training and during their ECT phase, and thankfully this situation is extremely rare. Induction tutors should ensure that appropriate support has been given before making this judgement.

Consider how you might address the following scenarios:

- The ECT arrives late to school.
- The ECT does not have professional clothing.
- The ECT is weak in several areas of their teaching practice but is not responding to advice. They are not following school policies.
- The ECT has inappropriate material on their social media account which might potentially bring the school into disrepute.
- The ECT is engaging in unprofessional gossip with other members of staff.
- You are supporting an ECT who is weak. Their parents ring the school and accuse you of bullying the ECT. The parents shout at you on the phone and later turn up at the school in a confrontational way.
- The ECT is going through the process of gender reassignment and needs time off for medical appointments.
- The ECT's absence record is beginning to concern you. They have already had 30 days absence this academic year and it is only March.
- The ECT does not agree with the school behaviour policy. They think it is too harsh and have told you that they do not agree with giving pupils sanctions.
- The ECT has missed some of their training sessions and stayed at home. However, the delivery partner has notified you.

- The ECT has dyslexia but is consistently making spelling mistakes on the board and in pupils' books and parents have started to complain.
- The ECT has told you that they have no intention of teaching long term. They are only doing it because they want the salary.
- An ECT develops chronic fatigue syndrome (CFS) and wants to go part time to manage the condition.

CASE STUDY

MANAGING BEHAVIOUR

Following a training session on behaviour management by the delivery partner, the mentor met with the ECT to link this training to the school context. The ECT was concerned about low-level disruption, particularly during times when pupils were supposed to be completing independent tasks. The mentor decided to organise some guided lesson visits to observe other teachers' practice. The focus of the lesson visits was to research how teachers minimised low-level disruption during independent tasks. Following the guided lesson visits, the mentor and ECT reflected on the strategies they had observed for managing low-level disruption. The strategies included:

- giving manageable, specific and sequential instructions;
- checking pupils' understanding of instructions before a task begins;
- using consistent language and non-verbal signals for common classroom directions;
- using early and least-intrusive interventions as an initial response to low-level disruption;
- reinforcing expectations about key transition points;
- consistently applying the school's behaviour policy;
- reinforcing established school and classroom routines.

The mentor and the ECT identified these strategies and linked them to the relevant '*Learn how to*' statements in the ITTECF.

CRITICAL QUESTIONS

+ What might the mentor do next?
+ What mentoring strategy is the mentor using in this scenario?

RESEARCH

Research suggests that teachers in the early stages of their careers are often challenged when the realities of teaching do not meet their expectations or when their personal beliefs about education do not match their workplace context (McKay and Manning, 2019). A strong teacher identity, developed during an ITE programme, can increase their capacity to respond to the professional challenges of teaching (Parsons et al, 2017). Teachers in the early stages of their career benefit from understanding the type of teacher they wish to become (Parsons et al, 2017).

Becoming a teacher is complex, messy and non-linear (McKay, 2013). Critically engaging with research and reflecting on their own values and beliefs will support professional growth and foster the development of a teacher identity (McKay and Manning, 2019). Strong teacher identities help teachers to navigate policy change (Dassa and Derose, 2017) and address professional challenges (McKay and Manning, 2019). Developing and nurturing the skill of critical reflection in the early stages of a teaching career can sustain teacher resilience (Greenfield, 2015; Mansfield et al, 2016).

SUMMARY

This chapter has introduced the role of mentoring when working with ECTs. It is important that ECTs have many opportunities to experiment with their teaching approaches, and mentors should encourage them to learn from both positive and negative experiences. ECTs are at an early stage in their careers. They should not be expected to 'hit the ground running' and they should be given time to learn about the kind of teacher they wish to be. Investing time in developing their teacher values and identity is not wasted time. Teachers with strong and stable identities are more likely to enjoy their careers and less likely to leave the profession. Government education policies do not always last long term. Focusing on how to implement a government policy alone may not provide new teachers with the tools to navigate a shifting policy landscape in education. Investing in developing a set of core professional values and beliefs which can 'stand the test of time' is more likely to pay dividends in the long term.

CHECKLIST

+ The ITTECF is not a curriculum because it is not sequenced and does not break down larger goals into small components.
+ The ITTECF is not an assessment framework: progress should be evaluated against the Teachers' Standards.
+ The ITTECF must be contextualised to the needs of the ECT and the school that they are working in.

FURTHER READING

Guidance for ECT mentors

Department for Education (DfE) (2022) *Guidance for Mentors: How to Support ECF-Based Training: Information for Mentors Assigned to Early Career Teachers (ECTs) Doing Training Based on the Early Career Framework (ECF) as Part of Their 2-Year Induction*. [online] Available at: www.gov.uk/guidance/guidance-for-mentors-how-to-support-ecf-based-training (accessed 28 March 2024).

Guidance on supporting ECTs

Department for Education (DfE) (2023) *How to Set Up Training for Early Career Teachers: Guidance for School Leaders and Induction Tutors on Setting Up Training Based on the Early Career Framework*. [online] Available at: www.gov.uk/guidance/how-to-set-up-training-for-early-career-teachers (accessed 28 March 2024).

CONCLUSION

This book has outlined some of the key developments in mentoring in the ITT/ITE context in England. It has also addressed the developments in mentoring in the early career phase. At the time of writing this book, we remain concerned about the increased expectations of school-based mentors in England. The requirement to complete significant additional training is a concern, given that mentors often hold school leadership responsibilities. Mentors are often carrying out the mentor role on top of senior and middle leadership duties, and mentors may be required to complete the additional training in their own time, alongside their other professional responsibilities. The funding that is available to support mentor release time does not cover all the time that mentors need to carry out the mentoring role, particularly if they are supporting trainees who require significant support. Within a policy context which is emphasising workload reduction and teacher well-being (Ofsted, 2024), the additional requirements for mentors seem at odds with the current direction of travel.

We remain concerned that the ITTECF (DfE, 2024a) does not differentiate between what trainee teachers are required to learn and what learning is required of early career teachers (ECTs). We are concerned that ECTs will be exposed to repetition of content and that this will result in significant additional workloads for new teachers during the first two years of their teaching careers. We are also concerned that the framework is reductionist. It privileges specific pedagogical approaches and 'cherry picks' the research which supports these approaches.

It is our view that trainee teachers and teachers in the early stages of their careers must be allowed to experiment with a variety of pedagogical approaches and supported to develop their own teacher identities. Becoming a teacher is complex, messy, and non-linear (McKay, 2013). Strong teacher identities help teachers to navigate policy change (Dassa and Derose, 2017) and address professional challenges (McKay and Manning, 2019). Literature suggests that teachers in the early stages of their careers are often challenged when the realities of teaching do not meet their expectations or when their personal beliefs about education do not match their workplace context (McKay and Manning, 2019). A strong teacher identity, developed during the ITE/ITT and ECT phases, can increase their capacity to respond to the professional challenges of teaching (Parsons et al, 2017).

Within this policy context, it is important that ITT/ITE providers are flexible in their approaches. Providers should develop training packages for mentors which do not result in increased workloads for mentors. Training can be delivered in person and online (synchronously or asynchronously), and providers should explore approaches for accrediting the work that mentors undertake. In addition, mentors require flexibility to allow them to shape the ITE curriculum in schools so that it meets the needs of trainees and ECTs. Developing strong models of partnership is important so that trainees benefit from a rich network of experienced expert mentors who can support their development. Developing greater synergy between centre-based training and training in schools is important to ensure that trainees receive a well-sequenced and coherent curriculum. Models of partnership which already exist and are well established between providers and schools will need to be further developed to accommodate the new legislative requirements.

Mentoring is a vital role. A skilled and supportive mentor can have a career-long impact on a teacher. Teachers never forget a good mentor, just as children never forget a good teacher. Good mentors do not want to produce 'carbon copy' teachers who are replicas of themselves. Teachers need to be empowered so that they can teach across a range of schools, in a range of age phases and across shifting policy contexts. Government policies come and go, but the nuts and bolts of teaching remain the same. Effective mentors nurture the development of principles, values and beliefs so that, regardless of inevitable policy changes, teachers can return to these and draw on them to navigate dynamic policy landscapes.

REFERENCES

Adams, G L and Engelmann, S (1996)
Research on Direct Instruction: 25 Years beyond Distar. Seattle: Educational Achievement Systems.

Aderibigbe, S, Gray, D S and Colucci-Gray, L (2018)
Understanding the Nature of Mentoring Experiences between Teachers and Student Teachers. *International Journal of Coaching and Mentoring in Education*, 7(1): 54–71.

Agarwal, P K, Bain, P M and Chamberlain, R W (2012)
The Value of Applied Research: Retrieval Practice Improves Classroom Learning and Recommendations from a Teacher, a Principal, and a Scientist. *Educational Psychology Review*, 24(3): 437–48.

Ashman, G (2019)
Explicit Teaching. In Boxer, A (ed) *The Research ED Guide to Explicit and Direct Instruction* (pp 29–36). Woodbridge: John Catt Educational.

Ball, S (2021)
The Education Debate. 4th ed. London: Policy Press.

Bambrick-Santoyo, P and Peiser, B M (2012)
Leverage Leadership: A Practical Guide to Building Exceptional Schools. San Francisco: Jossey-Bass.

Blazar, D and Kraft, M A (2015)
Exploring Mechanisms of Effective Teacher Coaching. *Educational Evaluation and Policy Analysis*, 37(4): 542–66.

Blazar, D, McNamara, D and Blue, G (2022)
Instructional Coaching Personnel and Program Scalability. EdWorkingPaper: 21–499. https://doi.org/10.26300/2des-s681

Burnette, J L, O'Boyle, E H, VanEpps, E M, Pollack, J M and Finkel, E J (2013)
Mind-sets Matter: A Meta-Analytic Review of Implicit Theories and Self-Regulation. *Psychological Bulletin*, 139(3): 655–701.

Cepeda, N J, Pashler, H, Vul, E, Wixted, J T and Rohrer, D (2006)
Distributed Practice in Verbal Recall Tasks: A Review and Qualitative Synthesis. *Psychological Bulletin*, 132(3): 354–80.

Chan, C (2020)
I Know How It Feels: How Online Mentors Help Pre-service Teachers Negotiate Practicum Tensions in the Third Space. *Mentoring and Tutoring: Partnership in Learning*, 28(2): 189–210.

Clark, C and De Zoysa, S (2011)
Mapping the Interrelationships of Reading Enjoyment, Attitudes, Behaviour and Attainment: An Exploratory Investigation. London: National Literacy Trust.

Clark, C and Rumbold, K (2006)
Reading for Pleasure: A Research Overview. London: National Literacy Trust.

Coe, R, Aloisi, C, Higgins, S and Major, L E (2014)
What Makes Great Teaching? Review of the Underpinning Research. London: Sutton Trust.

Coe, R, Rauch, C J, Kime, S and Singleton, D (2020)
Great Teaching Toolkit: Evidence Review. Cambridge Assessment International Education. [online] Available at: www.cambridgeinternational.org/Images/584543-great-teaching-toolkit-evidence-review.pdf (accessed 25 April 2024).

Creemers, B P M and Kyriakides, L (2006)
Critical Analysis of the Current Approaches to Modelling Educational Effectiveness: The Importance of Establishing a Dynamic Model. *School Effectiveness and School Improvement*, 17: 347–66.

Creemers, B P and Kyriakides, L (2011)
Improving Quality in Education: Dynamic Approaches to School Improvement. Abingdon: Routledge.

Daly, C, Hardman, M and Taylor, B (2022)
The Early Career Framework Pilots: Lessons Learned. In Ovenden-Hope, T (ed) *The Early Career Framework: Origins, Outcomes and Opportunities* (pp 95–112). Woodbridge: John Catt Educational.

REFERENCES

Dassa, L and Derose, D S (2017)
Get in the Teacher Zone: A Perception Study of Preservice Teachers and Their Teacher Identity. *Issues in Teacher Education*, 26(1): 101–13.

Davis, K D, Winsler, A and Middleton, M (2006)
Students' Perceptions of Rewards for Academic Performance by Parents and Teachers: Relations with Achievement and Motivation in College. *Journal of Genetic Psychology*, 167(2): 211–20.

Davis, P, Florian, L, Ainscow, M, Byers, R, Dee, L, Dyson, A, et al (2004)
Teaching Strategies and Approaches for Pupils with Special Educational Needs: A Scoping Study. Department for Education. [online] Available at: https://dera.ioe.ac.uk/id/eprint/6059/1/RR516.pdf (accessed 29 May 2024).

Deci, E L and Ryan, R M (1985)
Intrinsic Motivation and Self-Determination in Human Behavior. New York: Springer.

Department for Education (DfE) (1992)
Initial Teacher Training (Secondary Phase) (Circular 9/92). London: Department for Education.

Department for Education (DfE) (1993)
The Initial Training of Primary School Teachers: New Criteria for Course Approval (Circular 14/93). London: Department for Education.

Department for Education (DfE) (2018)
Factors Affecting Teacher Retention: Qualitative Investigation. Research Report. [online] Available at: https://assets.publishing.service.gov.uk/government/uploads/system/uploads/attachment_data/file/686947/Factors_affecting_teacher_retention_-_qualitative_investigation.pdf (accessed 28 March 2024).

Department for Education (DfE) (2019a)
ITT Core Content Framework. [online] Available at: www.gov.uk/government/publications/initial-teacher-training-itt-core-content-framework (accessed 25 April 2024).

REFERENCES

Department for Education (DfE) (2019b)
Early Career Framework. [online] Available at: https://assets.publishing. service.gov.uk/media/60795936d3bf7f400b462d74/Early-Career_ Framework_April_2021.pdf (accessed 25 April 2024).

Department for Education (DfE) (2021)
Initial Teacher Training (ITT) Market Review Report. [online] Available at: https://assets.publishing.service.gov.uk/media/60e45ae4e90e0764ce 826628/ITT_market_review_report.pdf (accessed 25 April 2024).

Department for Education (DfE) (2022)
Initial Teacher Training (ITT) Provider Guidance on Stage 2. [online] Available at: https://assets.publishing.service.gov.uk/government/uploads/system/ uploads/attachment_data/file/1119026/ITT_Provider_Guidance_Stage_2.pdf (accessed 28 March 2024).

Department for Education (DfE) (2024a)
Initial Teacher Training and Early Career Framework. [online] Available at: https://assets.publishing.service.gov.uk/media/65b8fa60e9e10 a00130310b2/Initial_teacher_training_and_early_career_framework_30_Jan_ 2024.pdf (accessed 28 March 2024).

Department for Education (DfE) (2024b)
Initial Teacher Training (ITT): Criteria and Supporting Advice. Statutory Guidance for Accredited ITT Providers. [online] Available at https://assets.publishing. service.gov.uk/media/65ccac0ec96cf300126a3718/2024-25_ITT_criteria_ and_supporting_advice.pdf (accessed 28 March 2024).

Department for Education (DfE) (2024c)
Evaluation of the National Roll-Out of the Early Career Framework Induction Programmes: Annual Summary (Year 2). [online] Available at: https://assets. publishing.service.gov.uk/media/65dfa86ff1cab36b60fc475f/DfE_ECF_ Report_Year2.pdf (accessed 28 March 2024).

Department for Education (DfE) and Department of Health (DoH) (2015)
Special Educational Needs and Disability Code of Practice: 0 to 25 Years Statutory Guidance for Organisations Which Work with and Support Children and Young People Who Have Special Educational Needs or Disabilities. [online] Available at: https://assets.publishing.service.gov.uk/media/ 5a7dcb85ed915d2ac884d995/SEND_Code_of_Practice_January_2015.pdf (accessed 28 March 2024).

REFERENCES

Dodge, R, Daly, A, Huyton, J and Sanders, L (2012)
The Challenge of Defining Wellbeing. *International Journal of Wellbeing*, 2(3): 222–35. doi:10.5502/ijw.v2i3.4

Donaldson, G (2010)
Teaching Scotland's Future: Report of a Review of Teacher Education in Scotland. Edinburgh: The Scottish Government.

Education Endowment Foundation (EEF) (2021a)
What Are the Characteristics of Effective Teacher Professional Development? A Systematic Review and Meta-Analysis. London: EEF.

Education Endowment Foundation (EEF) (2021b)
Cognitive Science Approaches in the Classroom: A Review of the Evidence. London: EEF.

Education Endowment Foundation (EEF) (2021c)
Metacognition and Self-Regulation. [online] Available at: https://educationendowmentfoundation.org.uk/education-evidence/teaching-learning-toolkit/metacognition-and-self-regulation (accessed 28 March 2024).

Education Endowment Foundation (EEF) (2021d)
Improving Behaviour in Schools: Guidance Report. [online] Available at: https://educationendowmentfoundation.org.uk/education-evidence/guidance-reports/behaviour (accessed 28 March 2024).

Education Endowment Foundation (EEF) (nd)
Communication and Language: Approaches and Practices to Support Communication and Language Development in the Early Years. [online] Available at: https://educationendowmentfoundation.org.uk/early-years-evidence-store/communication-and-language?approach=teaching-and-modelling-vocabulary (accessed 25 April 2024).

Education Policy Institute (2020)
Education in England: Annual Report 2020. [online] Available at: https://epi.org.uk/publications-and-research/education-in-england-annual-report-2020/ (accessed 28 March 2024).

Eldred, L, Gough, B and Glazzard, J (2022)
Male Pre-service Teachers: Navigating Masculinities on Campus and on Placement. *Gender and Education*, 34(7): 755–69.

Ellis, N J, Alonzo, D and Nguyen, H T M (2020)
Elements of a Quality Pre-service Teacher Mentor: A Literature Review. *Teaching and Teacher Education*, 92. https://doi.org/10.1016/j.tate.2020.103072

Engelmann, S (1992)
War Against the Schools' Academic Child Abuse. New York: Halcyon House.

Ericsson, K A, Krampe, R T and TeschRömer, C (1993)
The Role of Deliberate Practice in the Acquisition of Expert Performance. *Psychological Review*, 100(3): 363–406.

Feiman-Nemser, S (1998)
Teachers as Teacher Educators. *European Journal of Teacher Education*, 21(1): 63–74.

Fletcher, J, Astall, C and Everatt, J (2021)
Initial Teacher Education Students' Perceptions during a Practicum in Primary Schools: A New Zealand Experience. *International Journal of Mentoring and Coaching in Education*, 10(3): 298–316.

Gillett-Swan, J and Grant-Smith, D (2020)
Addressing Mentor Wellbeing in Practicum Placement Mentoring Relationships in Initial Teacher Education. *International Journal of Mentoring and Coaching in Education*, 9(4): 393–409.

Goldhaber, D, Krieg, J and Theobald, R (2020)
Effective Like Me? Does Having a More Productive Mentor Improve the Productivity of Mentees? *Labour Economics*, 63: 101792.

Gough, P B and Tunmer, W E (1986)
Decoding, Reading and Reading Disability. *Remedial and Special Education*, 7(1): 6–10.

Greenfield, B (2015)
How Can Teacher Resilience Be Protected and Promoted? *Educational and Child Psychology*, 32: 51–68.

Hattie, J and Timperley, H (2007)
The Power of Feedback. *Review of Educational Research*, 77(1): 81–112.

REFERENCES

Healy, G, Walshe, N and Dunphy, A (2020)
How Is Geography Rendered Visible as an Object of Concern in Written Lesson Observation Feedback? *The Curriculum Journal*, 31(1): 7–26.

Hobson, A and Malderez, A (2013)
Judgementoring and Other Threats to Realizing the Potential of School-Based Mentoring in Teacher Education. *International Journal of Mentoring and Coaching in Education*, 2(2): 89–108.

Izadinia, M (2016)
Student Teachers' and Mentor Teachers' Perceptions and Expectations of a Mentoring Relationship: Do They Match or Clash? *Professional Development in Education*, 4(3): 387–402.

Jacobs, L, Collyer, E, Lawrence, C and Glazzard, J (2021)
"I've Got Something to Tell You. I'm Dyslexic": The Lived Experiences of Trainee Teachers with Dyslexia. *Teaching and Teacher Education*, 104.

Jerrim, J, Sims, H, Taylor, H and Allen, R (2020)
How Does the Mental Health and Wellbeing of Teachers Compare to Other Professions? Evidence from Eleven Survey Datasets. *Review of Education*, 8(3): 659–89.

Jones, L, Tones, S and Foulkes, G (2019)
Exploring Learning Conversations between Mentors and Associate Teachers in Initial Teacher Education. *International Journal of Mentoring and Coaching in Education*, 8(2): 120–33.

Jones, L, Tones, S, Foulkes, G and Jones, R C (2021)
Associate Teachers' Views on Dialogic Mentoring. *Teachers and Teaching*, 27(1–4): 181–92.

Kirschner, P A, Sweller, J and Clark, R E (2006)
Why Minimal Guidance During Instruction Does Not Work: An Analysis of the Failure of Constructivist, Discovery, Problem-Based, Experiential, and Inquiry-Based Teaching. *Educational Psychologist*, 41(2): 75–86. https://doi.org/10.1207/s15326985ep4102_1

Knight, J (2007)
Instructional Coaching: A Partnership Approach to Improving Instruction. Thousand Oaks, CA: Corwin Press.

Knight, J (2017)
The Impact Cycle: What Instructional Coaches Should Do to Foster Powerful Improvements in Teaching. Thousand Oaks, CA: Corwin Press.

Land, C C (2018)
Examples of C/Critical Coaching: An Analysis of Conversation between Cooperating and Preservice Teachers. *Journal of Teacher Education,* 69(5): 493–507.

Locke, E A and Latham, G P (2002)
Building a Practically Useful Theory of Goal Setting and Task Motivation: A 35-Year Odyssey. *American Psychologist,* 57(9): 705–17.

Lofthouse, R M (2018)
Re-imagining Mentoring as a Dynamic Hub in the Transformation of Initial Teacher Education: The Role of Mentors and Teacher Educators. *International Journal of Mentoring and Coaching in Education,* 7(3): 248–60.

Mackie, L (2020)
Understandings of Mentoring in School Placement Settings within the Context of Initial Teacher Education in Scotland: Dimensions of Collaboration and Power. *Journal of Education for Teaching,* 46(3): 263–80.

Mansfield, C, Beltman, S, Weatherby-Fell, N and Broadley, T (2016)
Classroom Ready? Building Resilience in Teacher Education. In Brandenburg, R, McDonough, S, Burke, J and White, S (eds) *Teacher Education: Innovation, Intervention and Impact* (pp 211–29). Singapore: Springer.

Marzano, R J and Simms, J A (2014)
Questioning Sequences in the Classroom. *Marzano Resources.* [online] Available at: www.marzanoresources.com/questioning-sequences-in-the-classroom (accessed 25 April 2024).

McIntyre, D (1990)
The Oxford Internship Scheme and the Cambridge Analytical Framework: Models of Partnership in Initial Teacher Education. *Partnership in Initial Teacher Training,* 110–27.

McKay, L (2013)
Transforming Perceptions and Responses to Student Difference: The Journey of Seven Beginning Teachers. Unpublished doctoral dissertation. [online] Available at: http://eprints.qut.edu.au/62442 (accessed 25 April 2024).

REFERENCES

McKay, L and Manning, H (2019)
Do I Belong in the Profession? The Cost of Fitting in as a Preservice Teacher with a Passion for Social Justice. *Journal of Teacher Education*, 70(4): 360–71.

McLean, L, Taylor, M and Jimenez, M (2019)
Career Choice Motivations in Teacher Training as Predictors of Burnout and Career Optimism in the First Year of Teaching. *Teaching and Teacher Education*, 85(1): 204–14.

Mena, J, Hennissen, P and Loughran, J (2017)
Developing Pre-service Teachers' Professional Knowledge of Teaching: The Influence of Mentoring. *Teaching and Teacher Education*, 66: 47–59.

Mruk, C (1999)
Self-Esteem: Research, Theory and Practice. London: Free Association Books.

National Education Union (NEU) (2023)
NEU LGBT+ Inclusion Charter. [online]. Available at: https://neu.org.uk/latest/library/neu-lgbt-inclusion-charter (accessed 25 April 2024).

Nguyen, H T M and Hudson, P (2012)
Peer Group Mentoring: Preservice EFL Teachers' Collaborations for Enhancing Practices. In Honigsfeld, A and Dove, M G (eds) *Co-teaching and Other Collaborative Practices in the EFL/ESL Classroom: Rationale, Research, Reflections, and Recommendations* (pp 231–40). Charlotte, NC: Information Age Publishing Inc.

Office for Standards in Education, Children's Services and Skills (Ofsted) (2019)
Education Inspection Framework: Overview of Research. [online] Available at: https://assets.publishing.service.gov.uk/media/6034be17d3bf7f265dbbe2ef/Research_for_EIF_framework_updated_references_22_Feb_2021.pdf (accessed 29 May 2024).

Office for Standards in Education, Children's Services and Skills (Ofsted) (2020, updated 2024)
Initial Teacher Education (ITE) Inspection Framework and Handbook. [online] Available at: www.gov.uk/government/publications/initial-teacher-education-ite-inspection-framework-and-handbook/initial-teacher-education-ite-inspection-framework-and-handbook-for-september-2023 (accessed 28 March 2024).

Office for Standards in Education, Children's Services and Skills (Ofsted) (2023)
The Annual Report of His Majesty's Chief Inspector of Education, Children's Services and Skills 2022/23. [online] Available at: www.gov.uk/government/publications/ofsted-annual-report-202223-education-childrens-services-and-skills/the-annual-report-of-his-majestys-chief-inspector-of-education-childrens-services-and-skills-202223 (accessed 28 March 2024).

Office for Standards in Education, Children's Services and Skills (Ofsted) (2024)
Initial Teacher Education (ITE) Inspection Framework and Handbook. [online] Available at: www.gov.uk/government/publications/initial-teacher-education-ite-inspection-framework-and-handbook (accessed 28 March 2024).

Parker, A K, Zenkov, K and Glaser, H (2021)
Preparing School-Based Teacher Educators: Mentor Teachers' Perceptions of Mentoring and Mentor Training. *Peabody Journal of Education*, 96(1): 65–75. https://doi.org/10.1080/0161956X.2021.1877027

Parsons, S A, Vaughn, M, Malloy, J A and Pierczynski, M (2017)
The Development of Teachers' Visions from Preservice into Their First Years Teaching: A Longitudinal Study. *Teaching and Teacher Education*, 64: 12–25.

Pashler, H, Bain, P M, Bottge, B A, Graesser, A, Koedinger, K and McDaniel, M (2007)
Organizing Instruction and Study to Improve Student Learning. Washington, DC: U.S. Department of Education, National Center for Education Research, Institute of Education Sciences.

Platt, N (2022)
Spiralling into Control: Principles, Pivots and Pragmatism. In Ovenden-Hope, T (ed) *The Early Career Framework: Origins, Outcomes and Opportunities* (pp 115–32). Woodbridge: John Catt Educational.

Rohrer, D, Dedrick, R F and Stershic, S (2015)
Interleaved Practice Improves Mathematics Learning. *Journal of Educational Psychology*, 107(3): 900–8.

Rose, J (2006)
Independent Review of the Teaching of Early Reading. Nottingham: DfES Publications.

REFERENCES

Rosenshine, B (2010)
Principles of Instruction. *Educational Practices Series*, 21: 109–25. The International Academy of Education.

Rosenshine, B (2012)
Principles of Instruction: Research-Based Strategies That All Teachers Should Know. *American Educator*, Spring 2012: 12–20. [online] Available at: www.teachertoolkit.co.uk/wp-content/uploads/2018/10/Principles-of-Insruction-Rosenshine.pdf (accessed 28 March 2024).

Scheerens, J and Bosker, R J (1997)
The Foundations of Educational Effectiveness. Oxford: Pergamon.

Sherrington T (2019)
Rosenshine's Principles in Action. Woodbridge: John Catt Educational.

Sherrington, T (2020)
Top-Down Observation and Feedback Models Are Flawed: Time for Change. *Teacherhead*. [online] Available at: https://teacherhead.com/2020/01/25/top-down-observation-and-feedback-models-are-flawed-time-for-change (accessed 25 April 2024).

Sims, S (2019)
Four Reasons Instructional Coaching Is Currently the Best-Evidenced Form of CPD. [online] Available at: https://samsims.education/2019/02/19/247 (accessed 28 March 2024).

Skaalvik, E M and Skaalvik, S (2016)
Teacher Stress and Teacher Self-Efficacy as Predictors of Engagement, Emotional Exhaustion, and Motivation to Leave the Teaching Profession. *Creative Education*, 7: 1785–99.

Soares, A and Lock, R (2007)
Pre-service Science Teachers' Perceptions of Written Lesson Appraisals: The Impact of Styles of Mentoring. *European Journal of Teacher Education*, 30(1): 75–90.

Soderstrom, N C, Clark, C T, Halamish, V and Bjork, E L (2015)
Judgments of Learning as Memory Modifiers. *Journal of Experimental Psychology: Learning, Memory, and Cognition*, 41(2): 553–8. https://doi.org/10.1037/a0038388

Spicksley, K and Kington, A (2024)
Uniting Teachers through Critical Language Awareness: A Role for the Early Career Framework? *British Journal of Educational Studies*, 72(1): 23–41.

Spicksley, K and Watkins, M (2020)
Early Career Teacher Relationships with Peers and Mentors: Exploring Policy and Practice. In Kington, A and Blackmore, K (eds) *Social and Learning Relationships in the Primary School* (pp 93–116). London: Bloomsbury.

Stockard, J, Wood, T W, Coughlin, C and Rasplica Khoury, C (2018)
The Effectiveness of Direct Instruction Curricula: A Meta-Analysis of a Half Century of Research. *Review of Educational Research*, 88(4): 479–507. https://doi.org/10.3102/0034654317751919

Stonewall (nd)
[online] Available at: https://stonewall.org.uk (accessed 25 April 2024).

Sweller, J (1988)
Cognitive Load During Problem Solving: Effects on Learning. *Cognitive Science*, 12(2): 257–85.

Sweller, J, van Merriënboer, J J G and Paas, F (2019)
Cognitive Architecture and Instructional Design: 20 Years Later. *Educational Psychology Review*, 31: 261–92. https://doi.org/10.1007/s10648-019-09465-5

Taggart, B, Sylva, K, Melhuish, E, Sammons, P and Siraj, I (2015)
Effective Pre-school, Primary and Secondary Education Project (EPPSE 3-16+): How Pre-school Influences Children and Young People's Attainment and Developmental Outcomes Over Time. Research Brief. [online] Available at: https://assets.publishing.service.gov.uk/government/uploads/system/uploads/attachment_data/file/455670/RB455_Effective_pre-school_primary_and_secondary_education_project.pdf.pdf (accessed 28 March 2024).

Tereshchenko, A, Mills, M and Bradbury, A (2020)
Making Progress? Employment and Retention of BAME Teachers in England. London: UCL. [online] Available at: https://discovery.ucl.ac.uk/id/eprint/10117331/1/IOE_Report_BAME_Teachers.pdf (accessed 28 March 2024).

REFERENCES

Trevethan, H (2017)
Educative Mentors? The Role of Classroom Teachers in Initial Teacher Education: A New Zealand Study. *Journal of Education for Teaching*, 43(2): 219–31.

Vangrieken, K, Dochy, F, Raes, E and Kyndt, E (2015)
Teacher Collaboration: A Systematic Review. *Educational Research Review*, 15: 17–40.

Watson, J E and Johnston, R S (1998)
Accelerating Reading Attainment: The Effectiveness of Synthetic Phonics. *Interchange*, 57.

Weston, D (2020)
What Do Teachers Need to Know? Teacher Development Trust. [online] Available at: https://tdtrust.org/2020/10/22/what-do-teachers-need-to-know (accessed 25 April 2024).

White, E and Mackintosh, J (2022)
Educative Mentoring versus Instructional Coaching: What Approach Enables Mentors to Support Student–Teacher Learning? *Link* 6(1). [online] Available at: www.herts.ac.uk/link/volume-6,-issue-1,-april-2022/educative-mentoring-versus-instructional-coaching-what-approach-enables-mentors-to-support-student-teacher-learning (accessed 28 March 2024).

Wood, D, Bruner, J S and Ross, G (1976)
The Role of Tutoring in Problem-Solving. *Journal of Child Psychology and Psychiatry*, 17(2): 89–100.

Woolfolk Hoy, A and Spero, R B (2005)
Changes in Teacher Efficacy during the Early Years of Teaching: A Comparison of Four Measures. *Teaching and Teacher Education*, 21(4): 343–56.

Yeager, D, Walton, G and Cohen, G L (2013)
Addressing Achievement Gaps with Psychological Interventions. *Phi Delta Kappan*, 94(5): 62–6.

INDEX

NOTE: PAGE NUMBERS IN BOLD DENOTE TABLES.

- ACCREDITATION PROCESS, 7–8
- ADAPTIVE TEACHING, 38–40, 144–5
- AGE, AND INCLUSIVE MENTORING, 62
- AGE-PHASE CONSIDERATIONS, FOR MENTORS, 68
  all phases, 75
  Early Years Foundation Stage, 68–70
  primary phase, 70–3
  secondary phase, 73–4
- APPROACHABILITY, OF MENTORS, 128
- ART AND DESIGN, SUBJECT-SPECIFIC FEEDBACK, 89
- ASSESSMENT, 41, 99, 146
  conversations with pupils, 105–6
  documentary evidence, 104–5
  educational research, **119**
  lesson visits, 102–3
  professional discussions, 103–4
  through the ITE curriculum, 100–1
- AUTISM, TRAINEES WITH, 54
- BAMBRICK-SANTOYO'S SIX STEP MODEL, 26
- BEHAVIOUR
  behaviour curriculum, 42
  educational research, **119**
  management, 41–3, 75, 153
- BELIEFS, 154
- BRITISH EDUCATIONAL RESEARCH ASSOCIATION, 111
- CENTRE-BASED CURRICULUM, 31, 32, 33, 34, 157
- CHARTERED COLLEGE OF TEACHING, 111
- CLASSROOM PRACTICE, 36–8
- COACHING AND MENTORING, DIFFERENCE BETWEEN, 19
- CODE OF PRACTICE FOR SPECIAL EDUCATIONAL NEEDS AND/OR DISABILITIES, 38
- COGNITIVE COACHING, 25
- COLLABORATIVE RELATIONSHIP, SIGNIFICANCE OF, 18
- CONTENT KNOWLEDGE, 67, 79
  disciplinary knowledge, 80
  substantive knowledge, 79–80
- CONTENT-FOCUSED COACHING, 26–7
- CONVERSATIONS WITH PUPILS, FOR TRAINEES' ASSESSMENT, 105–6
- CONVERSATIONS, MENTORING, 146
- CO-TEACHING, 147
- COUNTING STRATEGY, 24–5
- CURRICULUM, 31
  adaptive teaching, 38–40
  ambitious, 45
  and assessment, 41, 100–1
  behaviour management, 41–3
  classroom practice, 36–8
  and ECTs, 147–51
  high expectations, 33–4
  and learning process, 34–5
  mentors' role and responsibilities, 45
  professional behaviours, 43
  and subject knowledge, 35–6
- DATA DASHBOARD, 100
- DECONSTRUCTION, 28–9, 126
- DELIBERATE PRACTICE, 22, 23
- DELIVERY PARTNERS, 143, 146
- DESIGN AND TECHNOLOGY, SUBJECT-SPECIFIC FEEDBACK, 90
- DEVELOPMENTAL FEEDBACK, 126
- DIALOGICAL APPROACHES, 20
- DIRECT DISCRIMINATION, 49
- DIRECTIVE APPROACHES, 19
- DISABILITIES, TRAINEES WITH, 53–4
- DISCIPLINARY KNOWLEDGE, 35, 65–6, 80
- DISCRIMINATION
  examples, **51**
  sex discrimination, 56–7
  types, 49, **50**
- DOCUMENTARY EVIDENCE, FOR TRAINEES' ASSESSMENT, 104–5
- DUAL CODING, EDUCATIONAL RESEARCH, 115
- DYSCALCULIA, TRAINEES WITH, 66

- DYSLEXIA, TRAINEES WITH, 54, 55, 66

- EARLY CAREER FRAMEWORK (ECF), 141, 147

- EARLY CAREER TEACHERS (ECTS), 141, 156

  approaches to mentoring, 146–7
  and appropriate bodies, 143
  and curriculum, 147–51
  and delivery partners, 143
  and induction tutor, 143–4
  minimum entitlement, 142
  professional challenges, 151–4
  role of mentor, 144–5
  roles and responsibilities of, 145

- EARLY READING, 71–3

- EARLY YEARS FOUNDATION STAGE, 68

  adult intervention in child-initiated learning, 68
  assessment, 68
  balancing adult-led and child-initiated learning, 68
  curriculum planning, 68
  early reading, 69
  enabling environments, 68
  rules and routines, 69
  sustained shared thinking, 69
  vocabulary development, 69, 70

- EDUCATION, HEALTH AND CARE PLANS (EHCPS), 39

- EDUCATIONAL RESEARCH, 110–11

  accessibility, 111
  challenges, 111–13
  introduction of teachers and trainees to, 111
  relevance to classrooms, 112
  summary of, **113–20**

- EDUCATIVE MENTORING, 46

- EFFECTIVE INSTRUCTION, PRINCIPLES OF, 14–15

- EFFECTIVE MENTORING, 18

- ENGLISH, SUBJECT-SPECIFIC FEEDBACK, 83

- EQUALITY ACT 2010, 49

- EXPECTATIONS OF TRAINEES, MANAGING, 138–9

- EXPERTS, MEETINGS WITH, 147

- EXPLANATIONS, EDUCATIONAL RESEARCH, 118

- EXPLICIT DIRECT TEACHING, EDUCATIONAL RESEARCH, 117

- EXTERNAL PROFESSIONAL DEVELOPMENT, 147

- FACILITATIVE APPROACHES, 19

- FLOURISHING, 130

- FOUNDATIONAL KNOWLEDGE, 34

- FUNDING, LACK OF, 156

- GENDER REASSIGNMENT, 57, 58

- GEOGRAPHY, SUBJECT-SPECIFIC FEEDBACK, 88

- GRADUATED APPROACH, 39

- GREENFIELD'S MODEL, 125

- GROUPING, EDUCATIONAL RESEARCH, 117

- GUIDED LESSON VISITS, 36–8, 67

- GUIDED PLANNING, 67

- GUIDED REFLECTION, 29

- GUIDED TEACHING, 67

- HEARING IMPAIRMENT, TRAINEES WITH, 54

- HINGE QUESTIONS, 28, 41

- HISTORY, SUBJECT-SPECIFIC FEEDBACK, 87

- HUMAN MOTIVATION, 131

- INCLUSIVE MENTORING, 48

  age, 62
  disabilities, trainees with, 53–4
  Equality Act 2010, 49
  lesbian, gay and bisexual trainees, 59–60
  pregnant trainees, 56
  race, 61
  religion, 61–2
  sex discrimination, 56–7
  trainees' needs, understanding, 53
  trans/transgender trainees, 57–9

- INDIRECT DISCRIMINATION, 49

- INDUCTION TUTORS, 143–4, 152

- INFORMAL CONTRACTS, 127

- INITIAL TEACHER TRAINING AND EARLY CAREER FRAMEWORK (ITTECF), 4–5, 9, 32–3, 45, 141, 156

  on content, 33
  on educational research, 110
  target setting, 107
  on trainee's minimum knowledge, 100
  training contextualisation, **148**

- INQUIRY-BASED COACHING, 25

- INSTRUCTIONAL COACHING, 20–3, 46, 126, 146

- INTENSIVE TRAINING AND PRACTICE OPPORTUNITIES (ITAPS), 10–14, 44

- INTERLEAVING, EDUCATIONAL RESEARCH, 115
- INTRINSIC MOTIVATION, 126
- LANGUAGES, SUBJECT-SPECIFIC FEEDBACK, 96
- LATER FRAMEWORK, 129
- LEAD MENTORS, 9, 45
- LEAD PARTNERSHIPS, 14
- *LEARN HOW TO* STATEMENTS, 5, 6, 32, 33, 147
- *LEARN THAT* STATEMENTS, 5–6, 32, 33, 147
- LESBIAN, GAY AND BISEXUAL TRAINEES, 59–60
- LESSON PLANNING, 146
- LESSON VISITS, 102–3, 126, 146
- LOCAL AUTHORITIES, 143
- MARKET REVIEW (2021)
  and accreditation process, 7–8
  overview, 7
- MATHEMATICS, SUBJECT-SPECIFIC FEEDBACK, 84
- MEETINGS, 106, 127
- MEMORY
  and content delivery, 5–6
  educational research, **114**
- METACOGNITION, EDUCATIONAL RESEARCH, 116
- MODELLING, 120, 146
- MOTIVATION, EDUCATIONAL RESEARCH, 119
- MUSIC, SUBJECT-SPECIFIC FEEDBACK, 92
- NEEDS OF TRAINEES, UNDERSTANDING, 53
- NON-BINARY PEOPLE, 58, 136
- OBSERVATIONS, 28, 34
- PEDAGOGICAL CONTENT KNOWLEDGE, 67, 78, 79, 81
- PEDAGOGICAL KNOWLEDGE, 67, 79
- PERSONAL, SOCIAL AND HEALTH EDUCATION, SUBJECT-SPECIFIC FEEDBACK, 95
- PHYSICAL EDUCATION, SUBJECT-SPECIFIC FEEDBACK, 93
- POVERTY, EDUCATIONAL RESEARCH, 113
- POWER IMBALANCES, 18
- PRACTICE, EDUCATIONAL RESEARCH, 114
- PREGNANT TRAINEES, 56
- PRIMARY PHASE, 70
  full primary curriculum, 71
  multiplication tables check, 71
  and nursery and Reception classes, 70
  progress monitoring, 71
  statutory assessment, 71
  subject content, 71
  synthetic phonics and early reading, 71–3
- PRINCIPLES OF MENTORING, 18
- PRIORITISATION OF TASKS, 134
- PROFESSIONAL BEHAVIOURS, 43
- PROFESSIONAL CHALLENGES, 151–4
- PROFESSIONAL CONVERSATIONS, 108
- PROFESSIONAL DISCUSSIONS, 103–4
- PROTECTED CHARACTERISTICS, DISCLOSURE OF, 53
- PUPIL ABSENCE, ADDRESSING, 75
- PUPIL PREMIUM FUNDING, 75
- QUESTIONING, EDUCATIONAL RESEARCH, 118
- RACE AND RACISM, 61
- READING CULTURE, 72
- READING FOR PLEASURE, EDUCATIONAL RESEARCH, 116
- READING LEADERS, 73
- REASONABLE ADJUSTMENTS, 54
- RECORDED LESSONS, 67
- RELATIONSHIPS, 127–8
- RELIGION, AND INCLUSIVE MENTORING, 61–2
- RELIGIOUS EDUCATION, SUBJECT-SPECIFIC FEEDBACK, 94
- RESEARCH CHAMPIONS, 111
- RESEARCH SCHOOLS NETWORK, 111
- RESEARCHED, 111
- RESEARCH-LED COACHING, 27

- RESILIENCE, OF TEACHERS, 125
- RETRIEVAL, EDUCATIONAL RESEARCH, 114
- SAFEGUARDING, 43, 75, 136
- SCAFFOLDING, EDUCATIONAL RESEARCH, 116
- SCHEMATA, EDUCATIONAL RESEARCH, 116
- SCHOOL-BASED CURRICULUM, 32, 33, 38
- SCIENCE, SUBJECT-SPECIFIC FEEDBACK, 85, 86
- SECONDARY PHASE, 73

  careers education approach, 74
  curriculum planning, 73
  opportunities to observe teaching, 74
  and sixth form observations, 74
  specialist subject, 73
  teaching opportunities, 73
  tutor time, 74

- SELF-ASSESSMENT, 108
- SELF-COMPETENCE, 132
- SELF-DETERMINATION THEORY, 130
- SELF-EFFICACY, 126, 146
- SELF-ESTEEM, 119, 131–2
- SELF-WORTH, 132
- SENCO, 38–9
- SEND, EDUCATIONAL RESEARCH, 118
- SEX DISCRIMINATION, 56–7
- SHERRINGTON, TOM, 23
- SIMPLE VIEW OF READING (SVOR), EDUCATIONAL RESEARCH, 116
- SPACED PRACTICE, EDUCATIONAL RESEARCH, 114
- SPECIAL EDUCATIONAL NEEDS AND DISABILITIES, 75
- STATUTORY ASSESSMENT TESTS, 41
- STRATEGIES FOR MENTORING, 146–7
- STRESS MANAGEMENT, 134
- SUBJECT KNOWLEDGE, 35–6, 76

  content knowledge, 79–80
  development in school placements, 66–7
  educational research, **113**
  importance of, 79
  pedagogical content knowledge, 79, 81
  pedagogical knowledge, 79, 81

- SUBJECT-SPECIFIC FEEDBACK, 67, 97

  art and design, **89**
  design and technology, **90**
  English, **83**
  geography, **88**
  history, **87**
  languages, **96**
  mathematics, **84**
  music, **92**
  personal, social and health education, **95**
  physical education, **93**
  religious education, **94**
  science, **85**, **86**
  synthetic phonics, **82**

- SUBJECT-SPECIFIC TARGETS, 67
- SUBJECT-SPECIFIC TUTORIALS, 67
- SUBSTANTIVE KNOWLEDGE, 35, 64–5, 67, 79–80
- SYNTHETIC PHONICS, 71–3, 74–5

  educational research, **115**
  subject-specific feedback, **82**

- TARGET SETTING, 107–8, 146
- TEACHER IDENTITIES, SIGNIFICANCE OF, 154, 156
- TEACHING SCHOOL HUBS, 143
- TEACHING SUPPORT, EDUCATIONAL RESEARCH, 120
- TEAM APPROACH TO MENTORING, 139
- THINKING PROMOTION, EDUCATIONAL RESEARCH, 118
- TRAINING MATERIALS, REVIEWING, 146
- TRAINING, FOR MENTOR, 9
- TRANS PEOPLE, DEFINITION OF, 58
- TRANS/TRANSGENDER TRAINEES, 57–9
- TRANSGENDER MAN, DEFINITION OF, 58
- TRANSGENDER WOMAN, DEFINITION OF, 58
- TRANSITIONING, 58
- TRANSPHOBIA, 59–60
- TUTORIALS, 104
- VALUES, 154

- **VIDEO-BASED COACHING, 24**
- **VISUAL IMPAIRMENT, TRAINEES WITH, 54**
- **VOCABULARY, EDUCATIONAL RESEARCH, 116**
- **WELL-BEING OF MENTORS, 137–9**
- **WELL-BEING OF TRAINEES, 139**
  context, 130
  individual factors, 126
  issues, 125
  relationships, 127–8
  see-saw, 133
  self-esteem, 131–2
  stress management, 134
  teaching challenges, 128–9
- **WORKED EXAMPLES, EDUCATIONAL RESEARCH, 115**
- **WORKLOAD MANAGEMENT, 134–6**

For Product Safety Concerns and Information please contact our EU
representative GPSR@taylorandfrancis.com
Taylor & Francis Verlag GmbH, Kaufingerstraße 24, 80331 München, Germany

www.ingramcontent.com/pod-product-compliance
Lightning Source LLC
Chambersburg PA
CBHW051526230426
43668CB00012B/1751